AF519435

Climate change forests and forest management

An overview

FAO FORESTRY PAPER

126

by

William M. Ciesla

Forest Protection Officer

FAO Forest Resources Division

1998

Reprinted by arrangement with the Food and Agriculture Organization of the United Nations

by

DAYA PUBLISHING HOUSE

DELHI-110035

Food and Agriculture Organization of the United Nations

Rome, 1995

"This book was originally published by the Food and Agriculture Organization of the United Nations (FAO) as Climate change forests and forest management-An overview, FAO Forestry Paper, 126".

"The designations employed and the presentation of material in this publication do not imply the expression of any opinion, whatsoever on the part of the Food and Agriculture Organization of the United Nations concerning the legal status of any country, territory, city or area or of its authorities, or concerning the delimitations of its frontiers or boundaries."

'The designations 'developed' and 'developing' economies are intended for statistical convenience and do not necessarily express a judgment about the stage reached by a particular country, territory or area in the development process.'

© Copyright 1995 by FAO
First Indian Edition, 1998
ISBN: 978-81-7035-209-9

Published by : **Daya Publishing House**
1123/74, Deva Ram Park,
Tri Nagar Delhi-110035
Phone 7103999
Fax : (011) 7198902

Printed at : **Replika Press Pvt Ltd**

FOREWORD

Changes in the world's climate, due to increases in the concentration of carbon dioxide and other greenhouse gases in the Earth's atmosphere, have the potential to significantly affect forests and the practice of forestry. The probability of climate change is one of today's leading environmental concerns. The issue is complex and filled with uncertainties. Information available on the subject is often confusing and conflicting.

Climate is the key factor which determines the distribution of vegetation. The relation of climate change to the conservation and development of the world's forests is therefore, an important issue to consider. Forests can contribute to the greenhouse effect, they can also be affected by climate change and they offer opportunities to mitigate its effects.

It is important for foresters to have an understanding of the climate change issue and its implications. This document, which is presented in question and answer format, is designed to serve as a general reference on the subject of climate change and forests. The answers are based on the current world's literature including the most recent analyses by the Intergovernmental Panel on Climate Change (IPCC). It is hoped that forest planners and managers will find it useful in the preparation and implementation of their programmes and in providing advice to decision makers.

J. P. Lanly, Director
Forest Resources Division
Forestry Department

ACKNOWLEDGMENTS

The helpful and constructive comments provided by a large number of people who reviewed this document is gratefully acknowledged.

External reviews were kindly provided by **M. Fosberg**, USDA Forest Service, Washington DC, **S. Brown**, US EPA, Corvalis, Oregon, USA and **M. Hosny El Lakany**, Desert Development Center, American University, Cairo, Egypt.

Internal (FAO) reviews were provided by **W.G. Sombroek**, Director, Lands and Water Development Division and Chairman, Interdepartmental Working Group on Climate Change; **R. Gommes**, Coordinator, Agrometeorology Group, Remote Sensing Centre; **J.P. Lanly**, Director, Forest Resources Division; **C. Palmberg-Lerche**, Chief, Forest Resources Development Service; **J. Ball**, Senior Forest Plantations Officer, **S. Braatz**, Agroforestry and Land Use Officer; **P. Vantomme**, Forest Management Officer; **D. Dykstra**, Forest Harvesting Officer (Presently with CIFOR, Bogor, Indonesia); **M. Trossero**, Wood Based Energy Officer; **C. Chandrasekharan**, Non-Wood Forest Products Officer and **D. Suparmo**, Advisor, Tropical Forests Action Programme.

Special thanks are given to **J.B. Harrington**, formerly of the Petawawa National Forestry Institute, Ontario, Canada, for his assistance with the technical editing of the manuscript and **F. Monti**, FAO, Forestry Department Librarian, who assisted in accessing the massive literature available on climate change.

TABLE OF CONTENTS

LIST OF ACRONYMS AND ABBREVIATIONS

C	Carbon
CFC	Chlorofluorocarbon
CH_4	Methane
CO_2	Carbon dioxide
ENSO	El Niño Southern Oscillation
FAO	Food and Agriculture Organization of the United Nations
FWD	Foundation for Woodstove Dissemination.
FTTP	Forests, Trees and People Programme
GCM	General Circulation Model
GEF	Global Environmental Facility
GHG	Greenhouse gas
Gt	Gigatonne (10^9 tonnes)
GWP	Global Warming Potential
ha	Hectare
IPCC	Intergovernmental Panel on Climate Change
IPM	Integrated pest management
NGO	Non Government Organization
N_2O	Nitrous oxide
NO_x	Nitrogen oxides

Pg	Petagramme (10^{15} tonnes)
ppbv	Parts per billion by volume
ppmv	Parts per million by volume
pptv	Parts per trillion by volume
tC	Tonnes of carbon
tC/ha	Tonnes of carbon per hectare
TCP	Technical Cooperation Programme (FAO)
TFAP	Tropical Forests Action Programme
Tg	Teragramme (10^{12} tonnes)
UNCED	United Nations Conference on Environment and Development
UNDP	United Nations Development Programme
UNEP	United Nations Environment Programme
USDA	United States Department of Agriculture
WB	The World Bank
WMO	World Meteorological Organization
WRI	World Resources Institute

LIST OF TABLES

LIST OF BOXES

LIST OF FIGURES

INTRODUCTION

The likelihood of global climate change and its possible effects, including its effects on forests, is one of the most hotly debated environmental issues of the decade of the 90s. Will the Earth's climate change in the future? The answer must be an unqualified **yes**. There have been alternating periods of cool and warm climate throughout our planet's 3.5 billion year history. Therefore, there is no reason to expect that the Earth's present climate, during which virtually all human development has taken place, will remain constant.

The more important and difficult questions are:

1. How will the Earth's climate change?

2. How will a changing climate affect the abilities of human societies to maintain and enhance their quality of life?

3. What actions can be taken to adapt to or mitigate the effects of climate change?

Many scientists argue that the present period of relatively mild temperatures which have dominated the Earth since the last great continental ice sheets began to recede some 10 000 years ago is a short interlude. They predict that another ice age will, once again, cover large areas of the Earth's surface.

A more near term concern is that the increasing evidence that certain human activities, such as burning of fossil fuels, conversion of forests to agricultural land at unprecedented rates and other activities are causing significant increases in the levels of carbon dioxide (CO_2) and other "greenhouse" gases in the atmosphere. These changes could lead to global warming at an unprecedented rate and could have serious implications for agriculture, fisheries, forestry and human development. Strategies for adapting to and mitigating the effects of an increased greenhouse effect are presently being considered at the national, regional and international level.

There is much confusion and uncertainty associated with the climate change issue. During the past decade, many studies, designed to improve our capacity to predict future climatic trends and the ways in which human society might be affected, have been conducted. The results of these studies are often conflicting and unclear.

The issues related to forestry are especially complex. Forests and human uses of forests can contribute to increases in atmospheric levels of greenhouse gases. Forests are also affected by changes in climate. In addition, trees and forests, because of their ability to absorb CO_2 and store carbon in woody tissue, offer an opportunity to help mitigate future climate change.

The complexity of forests, their relatively long life span and their multifaceted relationship with climate change pose many questions. How will forests be affected by climate change? How can foresters respond? Can forest management help mitigate the effects of climate change?

The purpose of this paper is to provide a broad overview of the climate change issue as it relates to forestry and forest management. It also attempts to provide some insights as to how foresters can respond to the challenges posed by possible future climate change. The material is presented in question and answer form in eight chapters. These focus on various aspects of the climate change issue including the dynamic nature of climate, the greenhouse effect, predictions of climate change and its effects, the global carbon cycle, forests as sources and sinks of carbon, the effects of predicted climate change on forests, strategies for helping forests adapt to climate change and the ways in which forests can mitigate the effects of climate change.

The material contained in this paper is designed for use by field foresters, programme managers and policy advisors at the national, regional and international level.

Chapter 1
THE EARTH'S CLIMATE - A DYNAMIC ENTITY

1. *HOW ARE WEATHER AND CLIMATE DEFINED?*

Weather is the atmospheric condition prevailing in an area at a given time, resulting in heat or cold, clearness or cloudiness, dryness or moisture, wind or calm.

Climate, as defined by the World Meteorological Organization (WMO), is the "synthesis of weather conditions in a given area as defined by long term statistics of the variables of the state of the atmosphere". Seasonal changes such as the transition from winter to spring, summer and autumn in temperate zones and from wet to dry in the tropics are also part of climate.

Climate is a key factor which determines the distribution of plants and animals and in the formation of soils through the weathering of geological materials and the decomposition or preservation of organic matter.

2. *TO WHAT EXTENT HAS THE EARTH'S CLIMATE CHANGED DURING THE COURSE OF GEOLOGIC HISTORY?*

While the Earth's climate has been sufficiently stable to support life for millions of years, climate is **dynamic** and subject to **change**. There is ample evidence from the fossil record and other indicators such as tree ring widths, growth rates of marine organisms and types of vegetation, as indicated by fossil pollen, that the Earth's climate has been characterized by periods of warm and cool weather ever since its existence (Fig 1.1). For example, over 230 million years ago, during the latter part of the Palaeozoic Era, glaciers covered much of today's tropics. During much of the Mesozoic Era, however, when dinosaurs and other reptiles dominated the Earth (180 million to 65 million years ago), temperatures were much warmer than they are today.

Over the past million years, the Earth's climate has been characterized by long periods of cold weather when continental glaciers covered large areas. Each of these lasted from 80 000 to 100 000 years and were interspersed by shorter periods of warmer weather which ranged from 10 000 to 15 000 years each. At the peak of the last glacial period, some 18 000 years ago, ocean levels were 130 m lower than they are today. The Bahamas were a substantial land mass during that time and the Sahel region of Africa was a desert. The continental glaciers began to retreat about 10 000 years ago. Some 6 000 years ago, as the glaciers were still in retreat, the Earth entered a period during which average temperatures were about what they are today but with slightly warmer summers and colder winters. Rainfall increased over the African Sahel and Lake Chad rose to more than 40 m above its present level. Human cultures in Africa were considerably more advanced than those in Europe. As the glacial ice sheets continued to retreat northward, the Sahel again became a region of marginal rainfall, with its northern regions invaded by the Sahara desert.

Many scientists believe that the present period of relatively mild temperatures which we enjoy today will eventually give way to another ice age (Easterling 1990, Harrington 1987).

3. *WHAT CHANGES HAVE OCCURRED IN THE EARTH'S CLIMATE SINCE THE BEGINNING OF RECORDED HUMAN HISTORY?*

Historical records show that over the past 1 100 years, the Earth has experienced swings in climate, at least on a regional basis, which have been sufficiently stable and have persisted long enough to be considered climate changes (Easterling 1990).

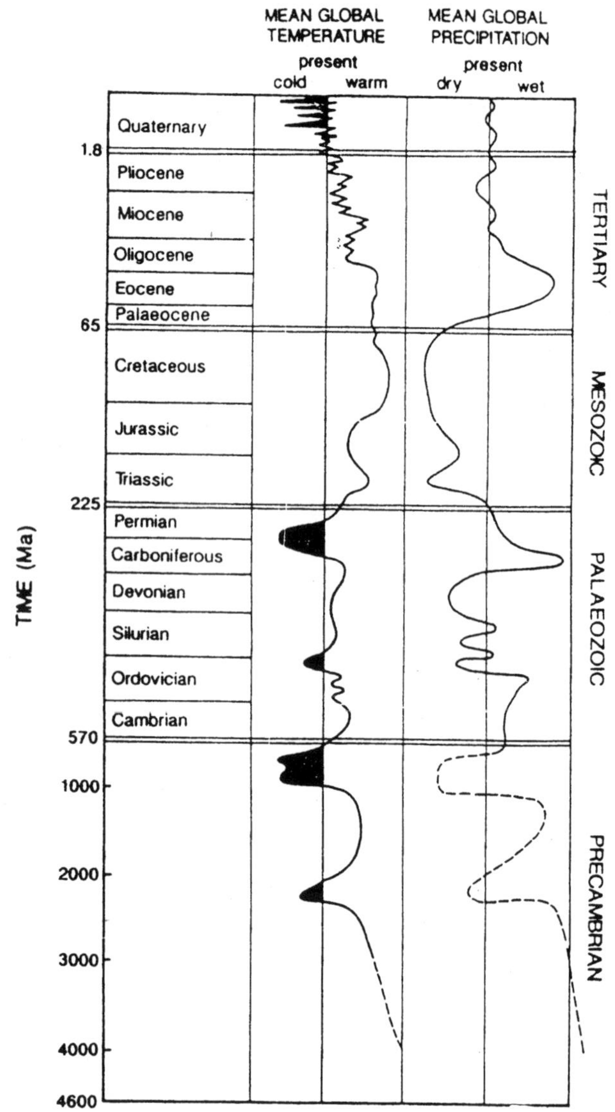

Figure 1.1 - A generalised history of changes in temperature and precipitation during geologic history. The curves indicate departures from today's global means. Periods colder than today are shaded. Dashed lines indicate sparse data (Source: Goodess et al (1992).

During the period in European history known as the Middle Ages, a warm climate, lasting from about A.D. 900 to A.D. 1200 dominated most of Europe and was known as the **Medieval Optimum**. This period allowed human habitation to extend into regions which would be considered climatically too harsh today. During the Medieval Optimum, oats and barley were grown in Iceland and vineyards flourished in southern England. Canadian forests extended north for a considerable distance from where they are today, agricultural settlements flourished in the northern highlands of Scotland and a Viking colony was established in Greenland.

The Medieval Optimum ended during the 13th century and was replaced by 600 years of pronounced cooling. As the cooling intensified, this period became known as the **Little Ice Age**. Snow and ice cover were more extensive during this period than at any time since the Pleistocene Period and its extensive glaciers. Viking colonies which existed in Greenland between AD 985 and 1500 died out (McGovern 1981). North American forests retreated southward and canals in Northern Europe were often frozen throughout the winter, bringing water transportation to a halt.

By the time the Little Ice Age lessened its grip on Europe's climate during the mid-1800s, various climatic parameters such as temperature and precipitation were beginning to be routinely recorded [1]. These data show that by the end of the 19th century, a warming trend began to occur in both the northern and southern hemispheres. This trend reached an initial peak during the 1930's. In the years immediately following, global temperatures cooled slightly before resuming their upward trend. The cooling trend was more pronounced in the northern hemisphere.

---

[1] Temperature and precipitation records for parts of Europe are available as far back as the 12th century. A summary of wet and dry summers in northern Germany is given by Finck (1985).

Box 1.1 **Historic droughts in California and Patagonia.**

While Europe was basking in the Medieval Optimum, other parts of the world apparently were suffering from prolonged drought. According to a recently completed study, which included analysis of ancient submerged tree stumps, the area of present day California, USA, was affected by two long and severe droughts during most of the Medieval Optimum. These were separated by a period of unusual wetness which lasted less than a century. The first of these droughts lasted for more than two centuries. The second persisted for over 140 years. There is evidence from the Patagonia Region of South America that it also was affected by drought during this time period.

The droughts in California may have been the result of a northward shift of summertime storms.

California is presently home to 30 million people. Consequently, a present day drought of this magnitude would be devastating (Stine 1994).

The world climatic record for the past two decades indicates that global surface air temperatures have increased above the 1930 maximums. This warming trend extends to both the Southern and Northern Hemisphere (Couglan and Nyenzi 1990) and has resulted in a global mean surface temperature increase of about 0.45° C since the middle of the last century.

4. *WHAT FACTORS CAN CAUSE CHANGES IN THE EARTH'S CLIMATE?*

Changes in the Earth's temperature and associated changes in climate have complex causes. These can be classified into the following categories:

> *Astronomical factors* - such as changes in solar activity, variations in the eccentricity of the Earth's orbit around the sun, changes in the tilt of the Earth's axis (obliquity) precession of the Earth's axis and collisions with asteroids or comets.
>
> *Geological factors* - such as continental drift, changes in the topography of the ocean floor, volcanic eruptions, mountain building, erosion and weathering of rock.
>
> *Oceanic Factors* - such as the El Niño effect, changes in ocean circulation, sea level changes, ice formation, phytoplankton blooms and dimethysulphide production.
>
> *Land Surface Factors* - including the effect of vegetation on surface albedo (the whiteness or degree of reflection of incident light from an object), and evapo-transpiration, open water effects including irrigation and dust.

Atmospheric Factors - such as the effect of greenhouse gases, sulphur dioxide and air pollutants, cloud effects and interactions between the air, the land and the sea.

Some examples of the influence of these factors on global climate are described in the following paragraphs.

Changes in solar activity, such as the frequency and intensity of sunspots, or the gradual warming of the sun as its supply of hydrogen is consumed, are believed to have significant effects on climate. The virtual cessation of sunspot activity for about 70-80 years in the 17th century, for example, coincides with the peak of the Little Ice Age, a period when a series of disastrous harvests in Europe resulted in decades of hardship and social unrest. The warming trend, which followed the Little Ice Age, coincided with a resumption in sunspot activity. The recent period of warmer temperatures, is associated with exceptionally strong sunspot activity beginning in the late 1980s (Harrington 1987, Windelius and Tucker 1990). However the measured increase in solar energy received by the Earth during peaks of sunspot activity does not appear to be sufficient to cause significant changes in climate.

In rare instances, large asteroids have collided with the Earth. Such a collision can have a number of catastrophic effects, including the development of a layer of fine dust in the atmosphere which reduces the amount of solar energy reaching the Earth's surface. This can cause reduced temperatures and light intensities. Some scientists believe that the collision of an asteroid of about 10 km in diameter with the Earth, some 65 million years ago, resulted in the drastic cooling that brought an end to the age of dinosaurs. Approximately one half of the genera of plants and animals living during this period became extinct (Harrington 1987).

The Milankovitch theory of ice age occurrence is based on long term variation in solar radiation received at the polar latitudes during certain seasons of the year. These are caused by changes in the eccentricity of the Earth's orbit around the sun, which varies between the limits of 0 and 0.06 with an average period of 93 000 years; the angle of tilt of the Earth's axis, which varies between 22.1 and 24.5° with an average of 41 000 years and the precession of the Earth's axis, which varies with an average period of 21 000 years (Weertman 1976).

Volcanoes occasionally erupt with such violence that large quantities of dust and gas are projected high into the atmosphere. Particles which reach the stratosphere may persist for several years. They cause cooler temperatures by reflecting solar radiation. The Little Ice Age was a period characterized by frequent volcanic activity when compared to the present century. The eruption of the Indonesian volcano, Tambora in 1815, the largest eruption in recorded history, was followed by a period of cool weather in portions of Europe, North America and possibly other parts of the world, known as "The Year Without Summer." This resulted in a failure of the corn crop in portions of the United States and massive crop failures in western Europe (Stommel and Stommel 1983). In Ghent, Belgium, for example, the summer of 1816 was the coldest recorded between the years 1753 and 1960 (Gommes 1980). Volcanic emissions due to the eruption of El Chichón in Mexico in 1982 and Pinatubo in the Philippines in 1991 also caused a slight cooling effect.

The ocean plays an essential role in the global climate system. Over half of the solar radiation reaching the Earth's surface is first absorbed by the ocean, where it is stored and redistributed by ocean currents before escaping into the atmosphere. The ocean currents are driven by the exchange of momentum, heat and water between the ocean and the atmosphere (Cubasch and Cess 1990).

An ocean current which is known to have a significant influence on global climate is known as El Niño (Spanish for

Christ Child). El Niño is a warm ocean current that typically appears along the coast of western South America around Christmas and lasts for several months. An El Niño is initiated by the Southern Oscillation (ENSO), which arises from the gradient between a low pressure system which lies over portions of Indonesia and Malaysia and a high pressure system in the South Pacific. When the difference in pressure between these two systems is reduced, the westward trade winds are weakened, causing a warming of the ocean surface off the coast of Peru. This causes the low pressure system to shift eastward and leads to a decrease in rainfall over Malaysia and Indonesia and increased precipitation over the west coast of Central and South America. A particularly severe ENSO during 1982-83 caused a severe drought on the island of Borneo resulting in the most extensive forest fires in recorded history. Approximately 3.5 million ha of primary and secondary rain forests in East Kalimantan, Indonesia were burned as a result of these fires (Goldammer and Seibert 1990). This same ENSO resulted in severe storms and massive flooding along the west coast of South America. ENSO events are known to influence weather worldwide. This is the principal global scale environmental factor which affects Atlantic seasonal hurricane activity. Hurricanes are suppressed during seasons when warm equatorial eastern and central Pacific water temperatures occur. Activity is enhanced during seasons with cold water climates (Grey 1993). There is also evidence that ENSOs are linked to below average rainfall in southern Africa (Cane et al 1994).

The oceans also contain chemical and biological mechanisms which are important in controlling CO_2. CO_2 is transferred from the atmosphere into the ocean by differences in the partial pressure of CO_2 in the ocean and the lowest layers of the atmosphere. The oceans also contain phytoplankton which convert dissolved CO_2 into particulate carbon which sinks into deep water (Cubasch and Cess 1990).

Box 1.2 Did the rising of the Tibetan Plateau cool the world?

The Tibetan Plateau, which lies between the Himalayas in the south and the Kunlun Mountains in the north is believed to have been caused by continental drift ending with India and Asia colliding. The Plateau covers about 2.2 million square kilometres and is equivalent to 0.4% of the Earth's total surface area. Average elevation is 5 kilometres above sea level. It has been suggested that the uplift of the plateau created patterns of air circulation which bring water laden air off the Indian Ocean in summer and deliver monsoonal rains to the Indian subcontinent. Atmospheric carbon dioxide is dissolved in the torrential rains, forming a weak solution of carbonic acid which erodes the plateau's bedrock and is delivered to the ocean as bicarbonates. This process is believed to have removed large quantities of carbon dioxide from the Earth's atmosphere resulting in a global cooling effect (Patterson 1993).

The average temperature of the Earth is presently 15°C. This is largely due to the effects of radiative or "greenhouse" gases which are present in the atmosphere. Without these gases, the Earth's average temperature would be -18°C. This is equivalent to the temperature of the surface of the moon and life, as we know it, would not be possible. Most of the short wavelength radiation which the Earth receives from the sun passes through these gases and warms the Earth's surface. The surface, in turn, emits long wave thermal radiation back to the atmosphere. This is absorbed by the greenhouse gases and heats the atmosphere. The atmosphere emits long wave radiation into space and downward to further heat the Earth's surface (See question 5 for a more detailed explanation).

Chapter 2
THE GREENHOUSE EFFECT

5. *WHAT IS THE "GREENHOUSE EFFECT" AND HOW DOES IT INFLUENCE THE EARTH'S CLIMATE?*

The greenhouse effect is the retention of heat in the lower atmosphere due to absorption and re-radiation by clouds and certain gases. The Earth receives its energy from the sun as solar radiation. Short-wave solar (visible) radiation received from the sun passes through the atmosphere with little or no interference and warms the Earth's surface. Long-wave thermal radiation emitted by the warmed surface of the Earth is partially absorbed by a number of trace or "greenhouse" gases (GHGs). These gases occur in small amounts in the atmosphere and reflect the long wave thermal radiation in all directions. Some of the radiation is directed downwards toward the Earth's surface (Fig 2.1).

The amount of GHGs in the atmosphere can influence global temperatures. If these gases were to increase, temperatures could rise. If they were to decrease, global temperatures would cool.

The greenhouse effect is a well understood phenomenon based on established scientific principles. The Earth's average surface temperature, for example, is warmer by about 33°C than it would be without the presence of these gases. Satellite observations of the radiation emitted from the Earth's surface and through the atmosphere confirm the effects of greenhouse gases. The composition of the atmospheres of Venus, the Earth and Mars are quite different but their surface temperatures are in general agreement with the principles of greenhouse effect. Finally, measurements from ice cores going back 160 000 years show that the Earth's temperature closely paralleled the amount of carbon dioxide and methane,

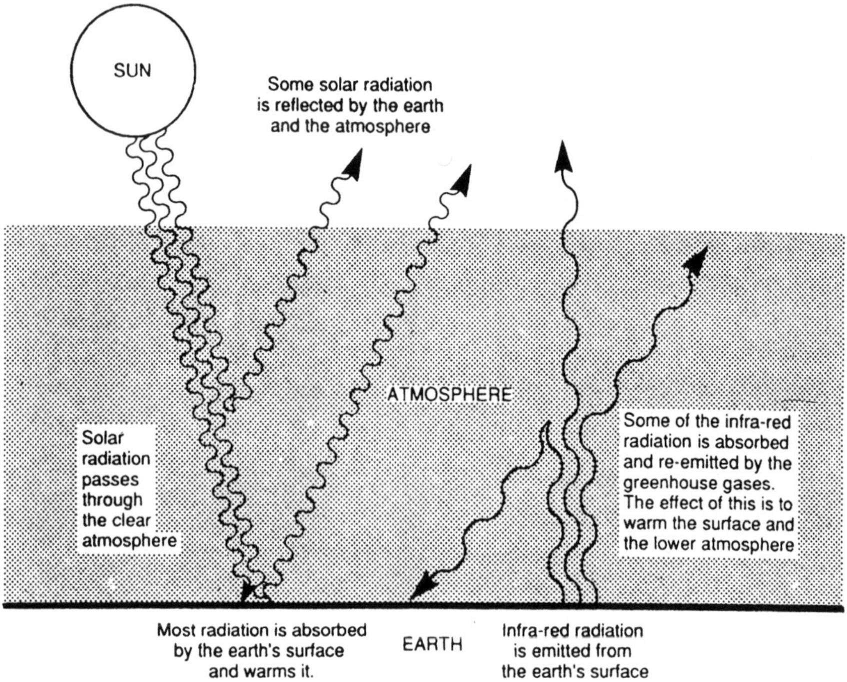

Figure 2.1 - A simplified diagram of the greenhouse effect (Source: Houghton 1991).

two of the more important greenhouse gases in the atmosphere (Fig 2.2). The changes in the amounts of these gases may be some, but not all, of the reason for the large (5-7°C) global temperature differences between the ice ages and the interglacial periods (Houghton 1991). Recent studies indicate that the temperatures and GHGs are so closely correlated that it is difficult to determine which is the cause and which is the effect.

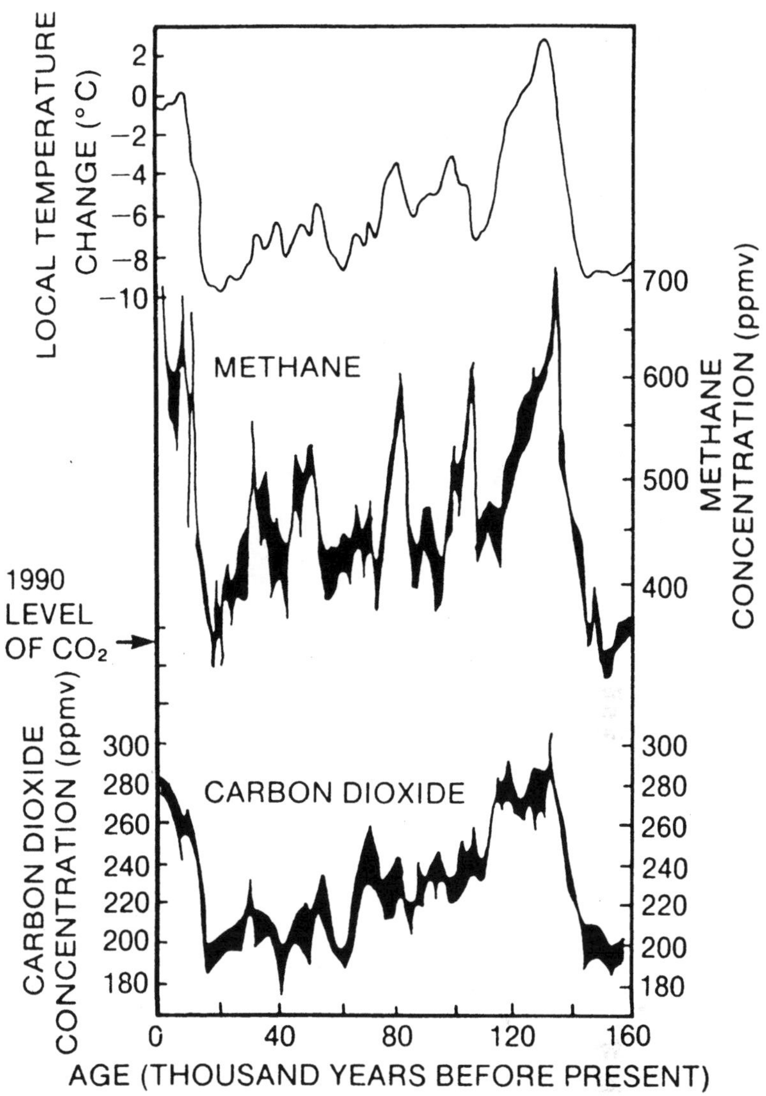

Figure 2.2 - Analysis of air trapped in Antarctic ice cores shows that methane and carbon dioxide concentrations were closely correlated with average temperatures over the past 160 000 years (Watson et al 1990).

6. WHICH GASES ARE CONSIDERED TO BE GHGS AND WHAT ARE THE SOURCES OF THESE GASES?

Greenhouse gases (GHGs) present in the Earth's atmosphere include **water vapour** (H_2O), **carbon dioxide** (CO_2), **methane** (CH_4), **nitrous oxide** (N_2O), **nitrogen oxides** (NO_x), **ozone** (O_3), **carbon monoxide**, (CO) and **chlorofluorocarbons** (CFC). The concentrations of these gases in the Earth's atmosphere have changed over geological time scales. Since the last glacial period, the levels of these gases remained relatively constant. As agriculture and animal husbandry developed, the world's population increased and human society became more industrialized, the levels of some of these gases increased significantly (Houghton 1991). Descriptions of the important GHGs and their sources are as follows:

WATER VAPOUR (H_2O) - Water vapour is the most abundant of the GHGs and has the largest greenhouse effect. The amount of water vapour is only slightly affected by human activities such as irrigation and development of reservoirs. The amount of water vapour will increase if the atmosphere becomes warmer. Increased amounts of water vapour could enhance the greenhouse effect.

CARBON DIOXIDE (CO_2) - Carbon dioxide is the most important of the GHGs influenced by human activity both in terms of the amount in the atmosphere and potential effects on global warming. This gas is a product of respiration by animals and plants, the burning of fossil fuels and the burning or decomposition of plants and trees. Cement factories are another important source of CO_2 (IPCC 1992).

Since the beginning of the Industrial Revolution, in the mid 18th century, the burning of fossil fuels has increased. Extensive deforestation and burning of debris has also occurred. These and other human activities have resulted in an increase in the concentration of carbon dioxide in the atmosphere by about 25% from 290 ppmv (parts per million by volume) to 355 ppmv at present. Most of this increase has taken place since 1940 (Hair and Sampson 1992). Recently a reduction in the rate of increase of atmospheric CO_2 has been detected (Sarimento 1993, see box 2.1).

METHANE (CH_4) - The major source of methane is anaerobic decomposition (decomposition by micro-organisms without the presence of free oxygen in the air). This occurs in rice paddies and natural wetlands. Methane is also a product of cattle and other ruminants, including wildlife whose digestive systems rely on enteric fermentation. Another source of methane is termites, which are present in large numbers in tropical forests (Zimmerman et al 1982). Other sources include biomass burning and decomposition from landfills and wetlands. Forest fires emit one unit of methane for every 100 units of carbon dioxide. The level of methane in the atmosphere has increased from 0.8 ppmv in 1850 to 1.7 ppmv at present. Since 1970, for reasons unknown, the rate of increase of CH_4 in the Earth's atmosphere has declined from about 20 ppbv/yr to as low as 10 ppbv/yr (IPCC 1992).

NITROUS OXIDE (N_2O) - This gas is emitted as a result of deforestation and associated burning, biomass burning, intensification of soil nitrification and denitrification processes in intermittently wet areas, application of nitrogen fertilizers and combustion of fossil fuels.

Box 2.1. What happened to atmospheric CO_2 levels in 1991 ?

According to data from the Mauna Loa Observatory in Hawaii, USA, a 35 year trend of steadily increasing levels of atmospheric CO_2 was broken beginning in mid-1991 when CO_2 levels were approximately 355 ppmv. By late 1993, a reduction of 1.5 parts per million (ppmv) of atmospheric CO_2 was detected. If this were applied to the entire northern hemisphere, it would equate to a loss of 1.6 Gt (1.6×10^9 tonnes) of carbon. This reduction in rate of CO_2 buildup began shortly after the eruption of the Philippine volcano, Mt. Pinatubo in 1991 and occurred despite the fact that an ENSO occurred during 1991-92. ENSOs normally result in a temporary increase in atmospheric CO_2.

The cause of this phenomenon is not known. Some scientists believe that a natural factor involving the oceans or the terrestrial biosphere is responsible. One possibility is that ash fallout, high in iron oxides, from the eruption of Mt. Pinatubo caused an iron fertilization of the oceans which temporarily increased their ability to absorb CO_2 (Sarimento 1993). If the Pinatubo eruption is the main cause, then the slowdown should be short lived.

Relatively little is presently known about the rates of release of this gas from soils in natural and disturbed ecosystems and from burning of biomass. The present level of N_2O in the atmosphere is about 0.3 ppmv and is increasing at the rate of 0.2 to 0.3% per year.

CARBON MONOXIDE (CO) - Carbon monoxide is not a true GHG. However it influences the oxidizing capacity of the Earth's atmosphere and thus contributes to increased concentrations of methane and nitrous oxides. Burning of savanna grasslands as a form of livestock and pasture management may be the largest single source because large quantities of CO are emitted as a result of incomplete combustion and smouldering rather than hot, rapid burning.

NITROGEN OXIDES (NO_x), SULPHUR DIOXIDE (SO_2). OZONE (O_3) AND CHLOROFLUOROCARBONS (CFC-11 and CFC-12) - These GHGs are the result of non-biotic, industrial processes such as the burning of fossil fuels, the chemical industry and certain household appliances. Forestry and land use practices are not sources of these GHGs.

Ozone is a gas which occurs throughout the atmosphere although most of it resides in the stratosphere where it acts as a protective shield and prevents harmful ultraviolet (UV) radiation from reaching the Earth's surface. In the lower atmosphere (troposphere) O_3 is formed as a result of lightning or as a component of photochemical smog. Exposure to elevated levels of tropospheric O_3 can cause damage to plants and be detrimental to human health. Certain varieties of beans and tobacco are known to be sensitive to elevated levels of O_3. Several species of trees can sustain injury as a result of exposure to elevated levels of this gas (Jacobson and Hill 1970).

CFCs, which were once used as aerosol propellants and are still used in air conditioning systems promote the destruction of stratospheric O_3 and contribute to its depletion. This is believed to cause seasonal ozone holes to appear over the polar regions.

7. *WHAT IS THE SIGNIFICANCE OF HUMAN SOURCES OF GHGS?*

Human activities are causing increases in the emissions of some GHGs into the atmosphere. Major human sources of GHG emissions include the burning of fossil fuels, deforestation (and associated burning) to make additional land available for agriculture and grazing and the burning of wood and charcoal. Approximately 7 Gt of CO_2 were released into the atmosphere each year during the 1980s from human sources (see question 23). Approximately 75-80% of this increase is due to industrial sources. Most of the remainder is due to deforestation and land use practices (Watson et al 1990). Other sources of GHGs include paddy rice production and animal husbandry. The latter two activities are sources of methane.

For over a century, scientists have warned that these increasing emissions may effect the atmosphere's radiative balance **leading to a significant and long-term increase in the Earth's temperature** (Plass 1959, Hepting 1963).

8. *DO ALL GHGS HAVE AN EQUAL WARMING EFFECT?*

No; GHGs vary both in the time they are present in the atmosphere before they break down (residence times) and in their radiative, or warming effect relative to carbon dioxide. Scientists have designated carbon dioxide the benchmark GHG against which the properties of all other GHGs are measured. In order to compare these gases, the concept of relative global warming potential (GWP) was developed as a means of accounting for differences in residence times and the radiative effects of GHGs (Table 2.1). Methane, for example, is a relatively short-lived gas, consequently emissions from this gas would have their greatest impacts on climate change during the first few decades after they are released. Nitrous oxide and CFCs, on the other hand, contribute to the greenhouse effect for hundreds of years because they are more stable and decompose very slowly in the atmosphere (IPCC 1992, 1994).

9. *WHAT EVIDENCE EXISTS TO SUPPORT THE IDEA THAT GHG LEVELS IN THE ATMOSPHERE ARE INCREASING?*

There is strong evidence that the levels of several atmospheric GHGs have increased over the past 150 years.

In 1958, the first continuous CO_2 monitoring programmes began at stations in Mauna Loa, Hawaii and Antarctica. Data from this monitoring clearly shows an annual increase in the mean annual concentration of CO_2. As of 1990, the global mean value was 355 ppmv. This is 25% above the 1850 value of 280-290 ppmv (Fig 2.3) (Houghton 1991, Siegenthaler and Sanhuezza 1991).

The concentration of methane in the atmosphere is presently 1.7 ppmv, more than double the 1850 value. Ice core analyses show that levels of this gas remained fairly constant during the 2000 years prior to industrialization. During the ice ages, the concentration of methane in the atmosphere was half of the present day level. Today's concentration of this gas is higher than at any time in the past 150 000 years.

During the 1980s, the rates of methane increase declined, dropping from 16 ppbv/yr in 1980 to about 10 ppbv/yr by 1990. Rates of methane buildup slowed dramatically in 1991 and 1992 but there are indications that they increased again late in 1993 (IPCC 1994).

TABLE 2.1

DIRECT GLOBAL WARMING POTENTIAL OF REPRESENTATIVE GREENHOUSE GASES FOR A 100 YEAR TIME HORIZON
(Source: IPCC 1992, 1994)

GHG	Global Warming Potential Relative to Carbon Dioxide
CO_2	1
CH_4	11
N_2O	320
CFC-11	4000
CFC-12	8500
HCFC-22	1700
HFC-134a	1300

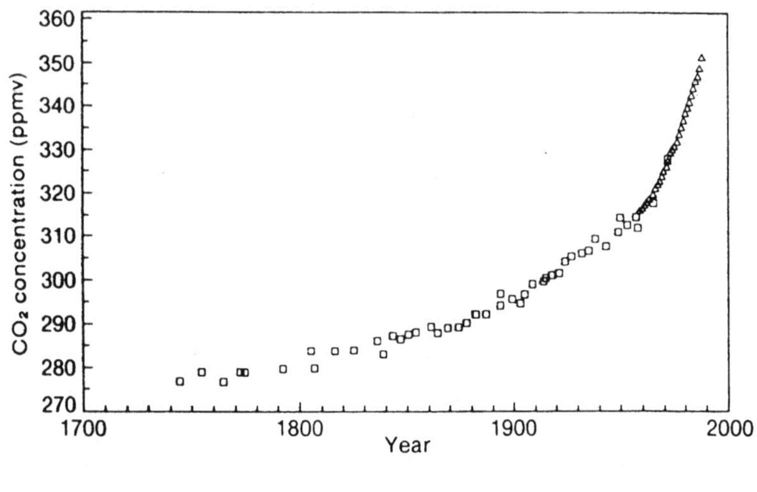

Figure 2.3 - Changes in the levels of atmospheric CO_2 over the past 250 years as indicated by analysis of ice core data from the Antarctic and by atmospheric measurements at Mauna Loa, Hawaii since 1958 (Source: Siegenthaler and Sanhuezza (1991)

The present day concentration of nitrous oxides is about 0.31 ppmv (parts per million by volume). This is 8% higher than pre-industrial times. CFCs are exclusively of human origin and are recent components of the Earth's atmosphere. They have been studied intensively not only because of their greenhouse effect but because they are depleting stratospheric ozone. In 1990, the atmospheric concentration of the two most important CFCs, CFC-11 and CFC-12 were 0.28 ppmv and 0.48 ppmv respectively (Houghton 1990).

10. WHICH COUNTRIES PRESENTLY MAKE THE GREATEST CONTRIBUTION TO ELEVATED LEVELS OF GHGS?

The ten leading contributors of GHG emissions are the USA, the former USSR, Brazil, China, India, Japan, Germany, UK, Indonesia and France. Many of these countries have a large industrial and service sector and burn large volumes of fossil fuels (Watson et al 1990). Developing countries (including China and the former USSR) accounted for 36% of the global energy related carbon emissions in 1990. This represents an increase from an estimated 28% in 1970 (Global Environmental Change Report 1994).

11. HOW CAN AEROSOLS COUNTERACT THE EFFECTS OF GHGS?

Aerosols consist of dust and other tiny particles which are released into the Earth's atmosphere. Many aerosols act as nuclei for the condensation of water droplets which make up clouds. Without condensation nuclei, clouds cannot form and rain could not occur.

There are numerous natural and human sources of aerosols. Dust from erupting volcanos or desert sand storms are two examples of natural sources. The black soot produced by forest, savanna and rangeland fires can be either a natural or human source depending on the cause of the fire. The most significant human source of aerosols is the emission of sulphates from power generating stations which can cause acid rain (IPCC 1994).

Aerosols may counteract the warming effect caused by elevated levels of GHGs. They help to cool the atmosphere in two ways. The primary effect is to scatter sunlight, reducing the amount that reaches the Earth's surface. An increase in the level of aerosols can alter the density and consequently the reflectance of clouds and cause a cooling effect. There is evidence from Australia, the United States and countries of the former USSR that the amount of cloud cover over these regions has increased. Consequently, some climatologists predict that some areas of the world may actually experience a cooling effect in the future (Pearce 1994).

Chapter 3
PREDICTED CHANGES IN THE EARTH'S CLIMATE AND EXPECTED EFFECTS

12. IN GENERAL, WHAT ARE THE PREDICTED EFFECTS OF INCREASED LEVELS OF GHGS ON THE EARTH'S CLIMATE?

Increases in atmospheric levels of CO_2 and other GHGs can have far reaching effects. They include increases in average temperatures and changes in precipitation, numbers of frost free days and the frequency and severity of storms (see question 15). There is also a likelihood that ocean levels may rise (see question 17).

Green plants utilize CO_2 during photosynthesis. Consequently increased levels of GHGs can have potentially significant effects on the growth and survival of green plants, including trees (see question 18). In addition, changes in climate could effect the distribution of animals and plants (see questions 33 and 34) and the processes involved in soil formation (see question 19). These effects could have serious implications in the future for agriculture, fisheries and forestry.

13. HOW ARE CHANGES IN THE EARTH'S CLIMATE PREDICTED?

The **general circulation model** or **GCM** is the most highly developed tool available with which to predict changes in the future world's climate. At least 12 different GCMs are now in use. These are based on the laws of physics and use descriptions of natural processes such as cloud development and deep mixing in the oceans. In the most recent GCMs, an atmospheric component, essentially the same as a weather prediction model, is coupled to a model of the ocean. Some of the more widely used GCMs are:

GISS -	Goddard Institute of Space Sciences
NCAR -	National Center for Atmospheric Research
UKLO, UKHI -	UK Meteorological Office
GFLO, GFHI -	Geophysical Fluid Dynamics Laboratory
CCC -	Canadian Climate Centre

To make a forecast of future climate, the model is first run over a simulated period of a few decades with no changes in the present atmospheric levels of GHGs. The statistical output is a description of the model's predicted climate which, if the model is a good one, will bear a close resemblance to today's climatic conditions. The exercise is then repeated with a new set of atmospheric conditions (e.g. the equivalent of a doubling of CO_2 levels, see question 8, Table 2.1). The differences between the outputs of the two simulations (e.g. mean temperature or inter-annual variability) provide an estimate of climate change (Fig 3.1). The long term change in surface air temperature following a doubling of carbon dioxide is used as a standard to compare predictions by different GCMs. The outputs are different between models which take an immediate doubling of CO_2 as a starting point when compared to transient models which apply more gradual increases in CO_2 concentrations.

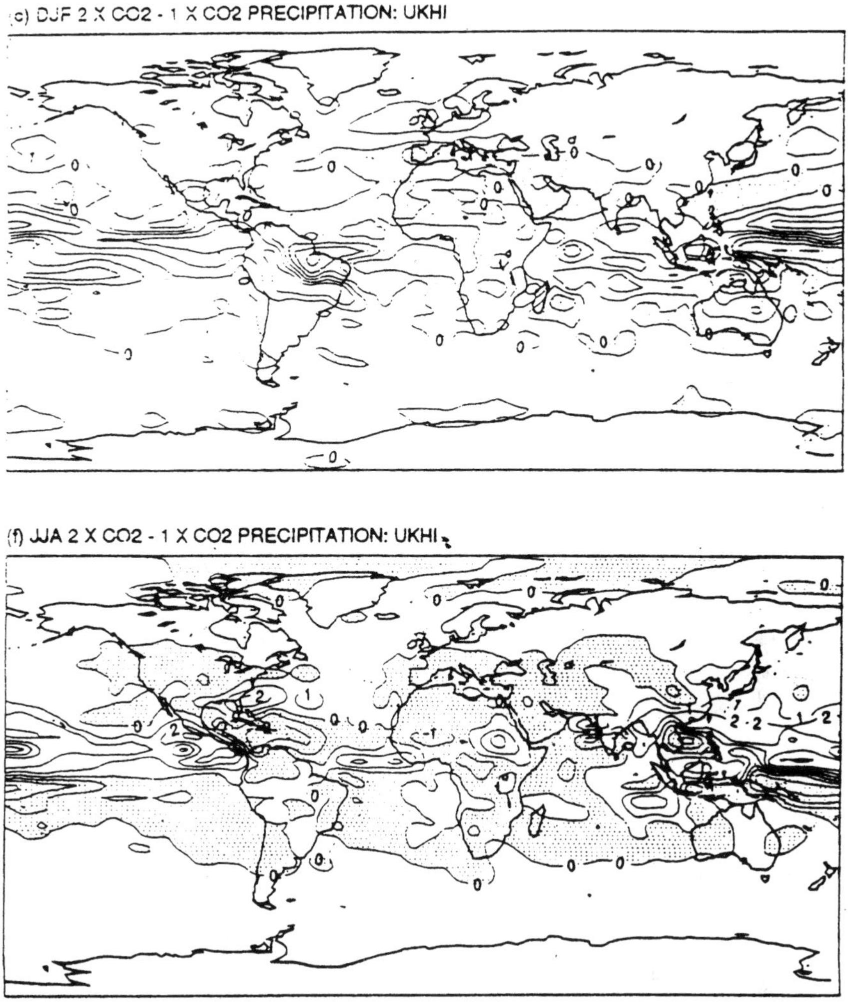

Figure 3.1 - An example of a prediction of global change in precipitation for winter (top) and spring (bottom) produced by the UKHI GCM. Areas of decrease are stippled.

Another approach to predicting future climate change is to search for periods in the Earth's past when global mean temperatures were similar to those at present or expected in the future. It is necessary for factors such as greenhouse gas levels, orbital variations, and other conditions such as ice cover and topography to be similar in order to get a good prediction using this approach. Periods in the Earth's history with levels of GHGs which are similar to today's or predicted for the next 100-200 years have not yet been found (Houghton 1991).

14. HOW RELIABLE ARE PRESENT PREDICTIONS OF CLIMATE CHANGE?

Predictions of climate change are uncertain because of our imperfect knowledge of future rates of emissions, the climatic response to these changes and of weaknesses inherent in the models used to forecast climate change.

Future climate changes will depend, among other factors, on the rate at which GHGs are emitted (see question 9). This will be influenced by a number of inter-related socio-economic factors. In addition, because of our imperfect level of knowledge of the sources and sinks of GHGs, there are uncertainties in the calculations of future concentrations arising from any emissions scenario entered into a GCM. Because natural sources and sinks of GHGs are themselves sensitive to changing climate, they could substantially modify future concentrations. For example, if wetlands were to become warmer, methane emissions could increase. If they were to become drier, more methane would be absorbed. There are also important processes in the oceans which can effect GHG concentrations (see question 4).

The models used to predict climate change are only as good as our understanding of the processes which affect climate. Presently this is far from perfect. The range of variability of climate predictions by different GCMs reflects model imperfections. The largest of these uncertainties is our understanding of the factors which affect cloud abundance and distribution and the interaction of clouds with solar radiation. Other uncertainties arise from the transfer of energy between the atmosphere and the ocean, the atmosphere and land surfaces, and between the various layers in the ocean (Maunder 1990).

Another point to keep in mind is that present GCMs describe the climate for an equilibrium situation (eg the situation arising from a doubling of CO_2 concentration in the atmosphere). They give no indication of how this equilibrium will be reached or how much time will be required to reach it.

15. WHAT CHANGES IN CLIMATE ARE PREDICTED WITH A DOUBLING OF CO_2 FROM PRE-INDUSTRIAL REVOLUTION LEVELS?

Based on outputs of several GCMs; temperatures are expected to rise, precipitation will generally increase, the climate may become more variable and there could be an increase in incidence of tropical storms. These changes are discussed in more detail in the following paragraphs.

TEMPERATURE - GCMs predict a range of temperature increase between 1.5 to 4.5°C with a doubling of CO_2 equivalents from level present during the middle of the 19th century. This is expected to occur at the rate of 0.3°C (± 0.2-0.5°) per decade during the next century and could result in a temperature increase of 1°C above present day levels by the year 2025 and of 2°C before the end of the next century (Houghton 1991). **According to some scientists, this rate of change is unprecedented in geologic history.**

PRECIPITATION - Increased warming of the Earth's surface will lead to increased evaporation and greater average global precipitation. However, some regions may have reduced rainfall. High latitude regions are expected to experience increased movement of warm moist air toward the poles, leading to increased annual precipitation and river runoff. Existing GCMs give widely different estimates of new geographic patterns of precipitation/evaporation ratios.

CLIMATIC VARIABILITY - Changes in the variability of weather and the frequency of extreme climatic events will generally have more impact than changes in the average conditions. However, with the possible exception of an increase in the number of intense showers, there is no clear evidence that weather variability will change in the future. Assuming no change in temperature range, but a modest increase in the average temperature, the number of days with very high temperatures could increase substantially. There could also be a decrease in days with very cold temperatures. Consequently the number of very hot or cold days could change substantially without changes in the variability of the weather. The number of days with a minimum threshold amount of soil moisture required for certain crops could be affected by changes in average precipitation (Houghton 1991).

STORMS - Tropical storms such as typhoons and hurricanes develop when ocean surface temperatures are in excess of 26°C. Higher ocean surface temperatures could therefore result in an increase in tropical storms and resultant damage including damage to forest resources (Fig 3.2). While systems are available to forecast storms in advance (Gray 1993), present day GCMs are unable to make such predictions. Consequently there is a great deal of uncertainty presently associated with the effects of climate change on storm events (Houghton 1991).

16. IS THE CLIMATE OF SOME REGIONS OF THE WORLD EXPECTED TO CHANGE TO A GREATER DEGREE THAN OTHERS?

Yes; there is general agreement among GCMs that there could be a broad latitudinal climate response due to an increased greenhouse effect. Warming could be much greater in the high latitudes and much less toward the equator. The most extreme temperature increases are likely to occur in winter in the high latitude of the northern hemisphere where changes could be a much as 2 1/2 times greater than the global average. The least amount of change is predicted to occur in the tropics.

Predictions of regional changes in climate are less clear. One study, which compares the predictions of several GCMs, indicates increased evaporation leading to increased summer dryness in mid-latitude continental interiors. Many of these regions are of great agricultural importance (Easterling 1990).

Figure 3.2 - Increases in the number of tropical storms, which can damage many resources including forests, are a possible, but uncertain outcome of global climate change.

17. WHAT CHANGES IN THE LEVEL OF THE OCEANS ARE EXPECTED DUE TO CLIMATE CHANGE?

An overall rise in sea level is predicted. This is based on the assumption that current rates of increase in the levels of GHGs continue as predicted. By 2100, a rise in ocean levels of 60 cm is expected. This is largely due to thermal expansion of the surface waters of the oceans. This could have severe effects on small island nations, countries with large areas of low lying coastal plains and where large population centres are concentrated in coastal regions.

A rise in the ocean level is not expected to be uniform over the entire globe. Thermal expansion, changes in ocean circulation and surface air pressure will vary from region to region as the climate changes. The magnitude of these changes is not yet known.

The most severe effects of sea level rise are likely to result from extreme climatic events, such as storm surges, the incidence of which could also be affected by a changing climate (Houghton 1991). This, however, is one of the less certain predictions of the effects of global climate change.

18. HOW WILL PLANTS, INCLUDING TREES, BE INFLUENCED BY CHANGES IN THE LEVELS OF GHGs IN THE EARTH'S ATMOSPHERE AND RESULTANT CHANGES IN TEMPERATURE AND PRECIPITATION ?

The changes in levels of GHGs in the Earth's atmosphere and expected changes in climate can have both **positive** and **negative** effects on plants.

One of the potential positive effects of increased levels of atmospheric CO_2 is known as the "CO_2 fertilization effect". It is known that CO_2 is a limiting factor in plant growth. Increased atmospheric CO_2 allows more photosynthesis by plants, resulting in at least a temporarily higher growth rate and rate of removal of atmospheric carbon by plants, provided that other requirements for plant growth are satisfied. Laboratory and field experiments indicate an increase in photosynthesis of about 30% in plants which use the C_3 photosynthesis process with increasing root/shoot ratios implying more underground storage of carbon [2]. An increase in the rate of photosynthesis of about 10% is expected in plants which use the C_4 process. It is likely that the gradual increase in atmospheric CO_2 over the past century has contributed partially to the approximate doubling of agricultural production worldwide which has been achieved largely through improved farming practices and genetic improvement of plant materials over the same period. Research trials indicate that this fertilizing effect would be most effective in the lower ranges of the CO_2 increase.

Related to the fertilizing effect is the fact that plants contract their stomatal openings at higher levels of atmospheric CO_2. This results in less water vapour loss and an increase in the plant's water use efficiency. This implies that increased plant growth may be possible in regions of the world where there is low precipitation. A study of the possible effects of higher water use efficiency by plants, combined with the CO_2 fertilization effect, indicates that the area where tropical rainforests could grow might increase by 75% with a doubling of atmospheric CO_2 and the area of deserts could shrink by 60% (Sombroek 1991).

---

[2] Most plants assimilate carbon by one of two photosynthetic pathways. These are commonly referred to as the C_3 and C_4 pathways. During the first stages of CO_2 absorption, C_3 plants manufacture a molecule with three carbon atoms and C_4 plants manufacture a four atom molecule. The C_4 molecule enables the plant to assimilate CO_2 more efficiently. C_3 plants depend on simple diffusion of CO_2 through their tissue and therefore benefit more than C_4 plants from higher CO_2 concentrations. Plants possessing the C_3 pathway account for 85% of all plant species and include all trees and woody plants. Plants with the C_4 pathway are tropical and temperate grasses which grow in areas of abundant warm season precipitation. Sugar cane, maize, sorghum and millet are all C_4 plants.

A higher global temperature implies a degree of increase in plant production, especially in high latitudes where the temperature rise would be proportionally greater according to the predictions of all GCMs.

Potential negative effects of changes in temperature and precipitation on plants include (FAO 1990):

* High daily temperatures, even of a few hours duration, can cause pollen sterility in some crops such as rice and wheat.

* Increased cloud cover and precipitation in some regions could result in reduced yields of many crops. Rice yields, for example, can be 1 to 2 tonnes less per hectare in rainy seasons than in dry seasons when grown under the same conditions.

* Areas with present day Mediterranean climates (mild, wet winters and hot dry summers) are predicted to become drier resulting in reduced soil moisture, especially during the growing seasons. This would result in reduced crop production, reduced growth rates in forests and increased risk of wildfires.

* The same conditions which result in increased crop yields will also favour weeds, enabling them to be more competitive with crops.

* Increased temperatures could cause pests and diseases to extend their ranges, particularly northward and into tropical highland regions. Survival of overwintering populations could be higher and breeding cycles shorter with consequent increases in the frequency and intensity of outbreaks.

* The areas where certain agricultural crops and tree species can grow may shift. One study indicates that climate change could result in a shift of several hundred kilometres of the North American corn belt from the Southwest to the Northeast (Easterling 1990). Depending on location, this could be both a positive and negative effect.

19. HOW MIGHT SOILS BE AFFECTED BY CHANGES IN CLIMATE?

Changing temperatures can alter the rate of microbial activity in soils. If temperatures increase, the rate of microbial activity will increase proportionally. This will cause organic matter to break down at faster rates, which in turn will accelerate the rate of CO_2 release. The amount of carbon stored in soils is estimated to be almost twice that in the atmosphere (see question 20). Consequently, a small increase in the rate of microbial activity can be expected to make a significant contribution to amount of CO_2 in the atmosphere. Some soils are also sources of NO_x and CH_4.

Breakdown of organic matter in soils results in a release of nitrogen and makes it available for plant growth. The rate of chemical weathering of mineral soil is also expected to increase with increased temperatures, making additional nutrients available for plant growth. Increased availability of soil nutrients could contribute to accelerated plant growth (Grace 1991).

20. IS THERE ANY EVIDENCE WHICH INDICATES THAT CLIMATE CHANGES MAY HAVE ALREADY OCCURRED DUE TO INCREASES IN GHG LEVELS?

In 1988, a drought occurred over the central portions of North America resulting in massive crop failures. This raised speculation among scientists and the general public that this drought was the result of an increased greenhouse effect. More recent climatic events, such as a drought over much of eastern and southern Africa which began during the 1991/1992 season and affected nearly 100 million people (Cane et al 1994), several severe hurricanes which battered the east coast of North America, the major flooding which occurred in the Mississippi and Missouri River Basins of the United States in 1993, and record high temperatures in Europe and North America in the early 1990s could also lead one to believe that the Earth is beginning to feel the effects of climate change.

Most climatologists insist however that there is not enough information to determine if these events are due to a changing climate or are part of normal climatic variation. Droughts, floods and severe storms have always affected human societies. At least one study indicates that the features of the North American drought of 1988 were consistent with droughts which occurred earlier this century. This would suggest that there is nothing new or particularly surprising about this drought. In fact, precipitation over the past decade in the Midwestern United States has been above normal, particularly during the summer, a trend contrary to that which some GCMs predict for an increased greenhouse response in this region (Easterling 1990). In addition, in 1988, the year of the North American drought, precipitation in the Sahel region of West Africa began to return to normal levels after a drought which lasted over 25 years (Gommes 1993).

Another complicating factor is that human populations have increased significantly over the past two to three decades. Consequently when climatic anomalies such as droughts occur, more people are affected. High human population densities also lead to less resilient agricultural production systems. This amplifies climatic anomalies. Land degradation, cultivation of marginal lands with low natural fertility or water holding capacity and shorter fallow periods can exacerbate drought conditions (Gommes 1993). This is especially true of regions such as Sudo-Sahelian Africa and northeastern Brazil which have been historically prone to drought events.

The average global temperature has shown a gradual increase of 0.3 to 0.5 °C since the 1850s. However this trend is so masked by annual and regional variations that it is virtually impossible to attribute the increase to a specific cause.

Chapter 4
THE GLOBAL CARBON CYCLE

21. *WHAT PROCESSES EXIST FOR THE EXCHANGE OF CARBON BETWEEN THE ATMOSPHERE, THE OCEANS AND THE LAND?*

There is a finite but extremely large amount of carbon on the Earth (Table 4.1). Carbon occurs in the ocean, in soils, fossil carbon reserves, bedrock, the atmosphere and plant biomass. The **carbon cycle** is the movement of carbon, in its various forms, between the Earth's surface, its interior and atmosphere. The major pathways of the exchange of carbon are photo-synthesis, respiration and oxidation. Movement occurs between living organisms, the atmosphere, the land and water (Fig 4.1). Over the course of millions of years, the carbon cycle has concentrated large amounts of carbon in bedrock, primarily as limestone and in fossil fuels.

The carbon cycle is thought of as four interconnected reservoirs or pools; the atmosphere, the terrestrial biosphere (including fresh water systems), the oceans and the sediments (including fossil fuels). The exchange rate of carbon between pools is referred to as **flux**. These reservoirs are either carbon **sources** and **sinks**. Carbon sinks absorb carbon from another part of the carbon cycle while carbon sources release carbon. For example, green plants absorb carbon from the atmosphere and are considered a carbon sink. An industrial plant which releases carbon in the atmosphere is considered a carbon source.

22. HOW ARE EXCHANGES OF CARBON BETWEEN RESERVOIRS EXPRESSED?

Exchange between reservoirs involves large amounts of carbon. This is expressed in multiples of metric tonnes. The units used throughout this paper are those widely used in the literature on climate change and carbon flux and are defined as follows:

1 teragramme (Tg)	=	10^{12} grams or 10^{6} tonnes.
1 petagramme (Pg)	=	10^{15} grams or 10^{9} tonnes.
1 gigatonne (Gt)	=	10^{9} tonnes or 1 Pg.
1 Pg	=	1 Gt.

Concentration of GHGs in the atmosphere are expressed as follows:

ppmv	=	Parts per million by volume.
ppbv	=	Parts per billion (thousand million) by volume.
pptv	=	Parts per trillion (million million) by volume.

TABLE 4.1

ESTIMATED DISTRIBUTION OF THE GLOBAL CARBON POOL (Source: Sombroek et al 1993)

Component	GtC
Oceans	38000
Fossil carbon reserves	6000
Soils	
Organic carbon	1200
Calcium carbonate	720
Atmosphere	720
Plant biomass	560-835
Total	47220-47495

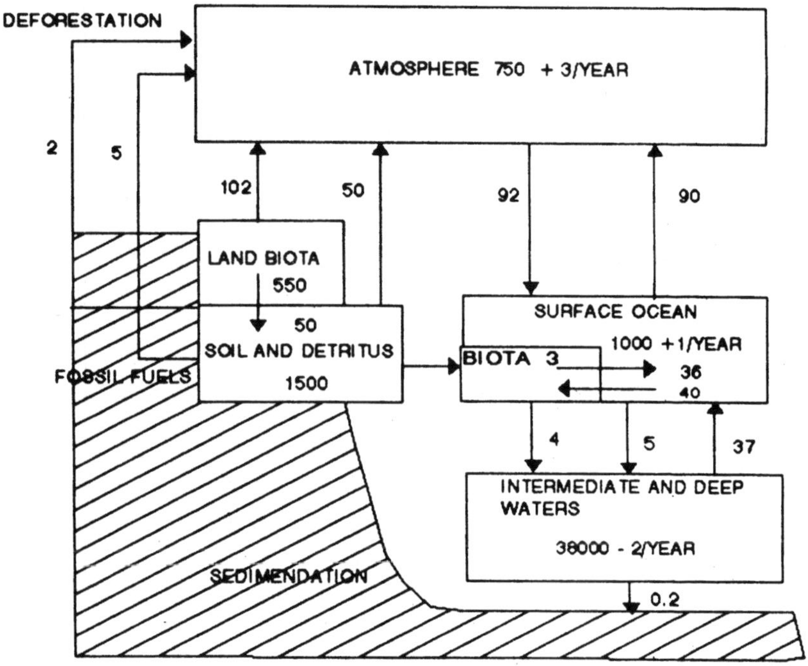

Figure 4.1 - Schematic representation of the global carbon cycle **showing movement of carbon (in Gt) between carbon sources and sinks (Source: Watson et al 1990).**

23. *WHAT IS THE PRESENT LEVEL OF CARBON EXCHANGE BETWEEN THE ATMOSPHERE, THE OCEANS AND THE LAND?*

According to estimates for the decade 1980-89, annual carbon fluxes due to CO_2 exchanges were as follows (IPCC 1994):

CO_2 sources:

Fossil fuel emissions	5.5 ± 0.5 GtC/yr
Net emissions from tropical land use (deforestation etc)	1.6 ± 1.0
Total emissions	7.0 ± 1.1

CO_2 sinks:

Accumulation in the atmosphere	3.2 ± 0.2
Uptake by the ocean	2.0 ± 0.8
Uptake by northern hemisphere forest regrowth	0.5 ± 0.5
Additional terrestrial sinks (eg CO_2 fertilization effect, nitrogen fertilization and climatic effects)	1.4 ± 1.5

The "additional terrestrial sinks" have not yet been quantified but are believed to be the primary components of the so called "missing carbon sink" which is yet to be accounted for.

Box 4.1 Peat Bogs - A major carbon sink.

Peat bogs could be a major additional component in the global carbon cycle. They are a natural store of carbon, holding between 500 and 1000 Gt of the element. This is similar to the amount stored in the world's trees and that which presently occurs in the earth's atmosphere.

Peatlands cover roughly 5 million km^2 of the earth's surface and range from the frozen tundra to the tropics. Large peat bogs in Sumatra and Borneo have accumulated peat to a depth of 20 metres over 8 000 years and hold up to 100 times the carbon per ha than the surrounding tropical rainforests (Pearce 1994).

Peat bogs can be a carbon source. In Ireland, peat is used as a fossil fuel. Also, during periods of dry weather, peat bogs can burn to great depths and smoulder for long periods. Peat fires are extremely difficult to extinguish.

Chapter 5
TREES AND FORESTS AS SOURCES AND SINKS OF GHGS AND CARBON

24. HOW MUCH OF THE EARTH'S SURFACE IS PRESENTLY COVERED BY FORESTS AND OTHER WOODY VEGETATION?

"Forests," according to the FAO definition, are plant communities where at least 10-20% of the surface area is covered by tree crowns. This accounts for roughly 3 459 million ha or about 27% of the Earth's land surface (FAO, unpublished data).

"Other wooded areas," are defined as plant communities where tree crowns cover less than 10-20% of the surface area and the vegetation consists mostly of shrubs, shrubby trees and thickets of woody plants between 0.5 and 7 meters in height. These areas include chaparral, scrub savannas and tropical thickets. These plant communities cover an additional 13% of the Earth's land area. Therefore, more than 40% of the Earth's land surface area consists of forests or other wooded areas (Table 5.1). More than half of these areas are located in the tropics.

The above estimates do not include agricultural lands where trees and shrubs serve as hedge rows, windbreaks or plantations of non-forest trees such as orchards, coffee, cacao, rubber and palm oil (Lanly 1989).

25. WHAT PROCESSES OCCUR IN TREES AND FORESTS WHICH CONTRIBUTE TO CHANGES IN LEVELS OF GHGS IN THE EARTH'S ATMOSPHERE?

Green plants remove CO_2 from the atmosphere through photosynthesis. The carbon is stored in the foliage, stems, root systems and, most important, the woody tissue in the

TABLE 5.1

LAND AREA COVERED BY FORESTS AND OTHER WOODED AREAS BY REGION (1980) (Source: Lanly 1989, FAO, unpublished data)

Region	Forests (%)	Other wooded (%)	Total (%)
Africa	18.0	21.3	39.3
Americas	37.0	15.2	55.2
Asia-Pacific	19.0	7.0	26.0
Europe *	27.0	8.6	35.6
WORLD	27.0	13.0	40.0

* Includes Russia

main stems of trees. Because of the long life span of most trees and their relatively large sizes, trees and forests are storehouses of carbon. Overall, forests store from 20 to 100 times more carbon per unit area than croplands and play a critical role in regulating the level of atmospheric carbon. The world's forests have been estimated to contain up to 80% of all above ground terrestrial carbon and approximately 40% of all below ground terrestrial carbon (soil, litter and roots). This amounts to roughly 1146 GtC. Approximately 37% of this carbon is stored in low latitude (tropical) forests, 14% in mid latitude (temperate) forests and 49% in high latitude forests (Dixon et al 1994).

When trees die or are harvested, the stored carbon is released. Some of the carbon becomes part of the organic matter component of forest soils where, depending on climatic conditions, it can remain for long periods. The remainder is released into the atmosphere, largely as CO_2 but also as CH_4 or other GHGs. The rate of release may be slow, as in the case of a single tree dying and being subject to years of breakdown and decay by fungi, insects, bacteria and other organisms. On the other hand, a sudden disturbance, such as a wildfire or clearing and burning of forests for agriculture and settlement by humans, can cause a rapid release of large volumes of GHGs into the atmosphere.

26. HOW MUCH CARBON IS RELEASED AND HOW MUCH IS TAKEN UP ANNUALLY BY FORESTS?

Estimates for the year 1990 indicate that the low latitude forests emitted 1.6 ± 0.4 GtC per year into the atmosphere, primarily due to deforestation. This is equivalent to approximately 23% of the total carbon emissions including the burning of fossil fuels. This was offset by a sequestration of 0.7 ± 0.2 GtC per year by forest expansion and growth in the mid and high latitudes (Table 5.2). Consequently, there is presently a net carbon **contribution** of 0.9 ± 0.4 GtC per year to the atmosphere from the world's forest ecosystems (Dixon et al 1994). This is undoubtedly due to increased rates of tropical deforestation during the decade of the 1980s (see question 25). At the beginning of the decade, the estimated accumulation of carbon in recovering tropical landscapes which had previously been disturbed was roughly equal to net carbon emissions due to tropical deforestation and associated burning (Lugo and Brown 1992).

27. DO DIFFERENT FOREST ECOSYSTEMS VARY IN THEIR CAPACITY TO ABSORB AND STORE CARBON?

Forests vary considerably in their capacity to absorb and store carbon. Factors which influence carbon absorption rates include temperature, precipitation, stocking, soil, slope, elevation, site conditions, growth rates and age. Generally speaking, closed forests have a greater capacity to store carbon than open forests and woodlands. Undisturbed forests store more carbon than degraded forests. Wet or moist

TABLE 5.2

ESTIMATED ANNUAL RATES OF CARBON EXCHANGE BETWEEN THE WORLD'S FORESTS AND THE ATMOSPHERE

Latitudinal Belt	Carbon Exchange (Gt/Year) ***
High	
Russia	+0.30 to +0.50
Canada	+0.08
Subtotal	+0.48 ±0.1
Mid	
USA*	+0.10 to +0.25
Europe**	+0.09 to +0.12
China	-0.02
Australia	trace
Subtotal	+0.26 ±0.09
Low	
Asia	-0.50 to -0.90
Africa	-0.25 to -0.45
Americas	-0.50 to -0.70
Subtotal	-1.65 ± 0.40
Total	-0.9 ± 0.4

* Includes continental USA and Alaska.
** Includes Nordic countries
*** + Indicates transfer from atmosphere to forest.
- Indicates transfer from forest to atmosphere.

Source: Dixon et al 1994

forests store more carbon than dry or semi-arid forests and mature forests store greater quantities of carbon than do young forests.

Many studies have been conducted to estimate the biomass of forest ecosystems. These can be used to estimate carbon storage. The ratio of dry total biomass to carbon is roughly 2:1. The carbon content of an undisturbed tropical moist forest can range has high as 250 tC/ha of standing, above ground biomass. The carbon content of tropical, dry forests with open, discontinuous canopies, on the other hand, generally averages less than 40 tC/ha (Brown and Lugo 1984) (Table 5.3).

Forest soils also store carbon. A recent study indicates that 84.3% of the total carbon content of high latitude forests is stored in the soil. For mid-latitude forests, 63% is stored in the soil and for low latitude forests, the proportion is 50.4% (Dixon et al 1994) (Table 5.4).

28. DO TREES AND FORESTS REMOVE CARBON FROM THE EARTH'S ATMOSPHERE AT DIFFERENT RATES DURING DIFFERENT STAGES IN THEIR LIVES?

The rate of carbon absorption by trees and forests is a function of growth rates and age. Generally speaking, trees and forests remove atmospheric carbon at high rates when they are young and fast growing. As stands approach maturity and growth rates are reduced, the net carbon absorption is also reduced. In theory, mature forests reach a stage of equilibrium with respect to carbon absorption. Roughly an equal amount of carbon is released through decay of dead and diseased trees as is absorbed. However this is rarely achieved in natural forests. Mature forests, if left undisturbed, as is the case in reserved or protected forests, are carbon reservoirs but not necessarily net carbon sinks.

TABLE 5.3

ESTIMATES OF AVERAGE ABOVE GROUND STORED CARBON/HA BY VARIOUS VEGETATION COMMUNITIES
(Based on biomass values from Olsen et al(1983))

Holdridge Life Zone	tC/ha
Forest	
Tropical wet	100
Tropical moist	70
Tropical dry	50
Subtropical wet	65
Subtropical moist	35
Warm temperate	50
Warm dry temperate	25
Cool temperate	50
Wet boreal	55
Moist boreal	40
Non Forest	
Tropical thorn woodland	15
Temperate thorn steppe	8
Cool temperate steppe	5
Tropical desert bush	2
Temperate desert bush	3
Boreal desert	5
Tundra	2.5

TABLE 5.4

ESTIMATED CARBON DENSITIES PER UNIT OF FOREST AREA IN VEGETATION AND SOILS OF THE WORLD'S FORESTS

Latitudinal Belt	Carbon Densities (tC/ha)	
	Vegetation	Soils
High		
Russia	83	281
Canada	28	484
Alaska	39	212
Mean	64 (15.7%)	343 (84.3%)
Mid		
USA	62	108
Europe*	32	90
China	114	136
Australia	45	83
Mean	57 (37%)	96 (63%)
Low		
Asia	132-174	139
Africa	99	120
Americas	130	120
Mean	121 (49.6%)	123 (50.4%)

* Includes Nordic countries.

Source: Dixon et al 1994.

Box 5.1 **The role of forest plantations in New Zealand's carbon balance.**

According to estimates made by a team of research scientists in New Zealand, the country's 1.24 million ha of plantation forests absorbed 4.5 ± 0.8 million tonnes of carbon between 1 April 1988 and 1 April 1989. The total above ground carbon stored in New Zealand's forest plantation estate is approximately 88 million tonnes.

Carbon absorption by New Zealand's forest plantations for the period studied was equivalent to approximately 70% of the country's fossil fuel emissions but <0.1% of the total global fossil fuel emissions.

The high annual rate of carbon uptake by these plantations is a consequence of the large area of new plantings established during the 1970s and 1980s. Without continued new plantings, the net annual rate of carbon absorption of these plantations will rapidly approach zero (Hollinger et al 1993) .

Studies of carbon absorption rates in tropical forest plantations indicate that maximum growth and carbon uptake occurs during age classes 0-5 and 6-10 years (62%). Carbon uptake decreases by about 50% during the next 5 years and decreases even further after age 16 (Brown et al 1986).29.

29. *WHICH HUMAN ACTIVITIES IN FORESTS AND WOODLANDS CONTRIBUTE TO INCREASES IN THE LEVELS OF GHGS?*

DEFORESTATION - Felling and burning of forests to make land available for agriculture or livestock grazing, is the major forest sector contributor to increases in the levels of GHGs and is the second largest human caused source of GHGs

Human societies have been cutting forests for millennia. Until the early part of this century, deforestation occurred mainly in temperate forests. More recently, it has been concentrated in the tropics. Deforestation, and associated burning, results in a massive and rapid release of carbon into the atmosphere, primarily as CO_2. Smaller amounts of CH_4 and CO are also emitted. Tropical forests play an important role in the global carbon cycle because they store about 50% of the world's living terrestrial carbon (Dixon et al 1994). High rates of deforestation in the tropics is the reason that forests presently make a net contribution to atmospheric carbon, despite the fact that they are able to store large quantities of carbon.

Deforestation can also alter climate directly by increasing reflectivity (albedo) and decreasing evapo-transpiration. Experiments with climate models predict that the replacement of all of the forests of the Amazon Basin with grassland would reduce the rainfall over the basin by about 20% and increase the average regional temperature by several degrees (Maunder 1990).

BIOMASS BURNING - The term "biomass burning" includes all intentional human activities associated with forest clearing, the burning of savanna vegetation to stimulate regeneration of grasses for livestock, burning of fuel wood and charcoal and consumption of agricultural residues. The area of savanna vegetation burned each year is estimated at 750 million ha. About half of this area is in Africa (Fig 5.1). Shifting cultivation, a practice in which the natural vegetation is cleared, used for agriculture for 2 to 5 years and then allowed to remain fallow and revegetate with natural vegetation for 7 to 12 years before being cleared again, is practised by 200 million people world wide on 300 to 500 million ha. Approximately 87% of the biomass burning occurs in the tropics.

WILDFIRES - A "wildfire" is defined as any fire occurring on wild (undeveloped) lands except a fire under prescription (one which is set intentionally) (FAO 1986). Recent estimates indicate that between 12 and 13 million ha of forests and other wooded lands are burned annually (Calabri and Ciesla 1992). With the exception of remote forest areas in portions of North America and Siberia, most forest and other wildland fires are of human origin. Human causes of wildfires include escaped prescribed fires, carelessness, and arson. Natural causes of wildfires are lightning storms, volcanic activity and burning of underground peat and coal deposits.

OTHER ACTIVITIES - Other human activities connected with forests and forest products which contribute to elevated levels of greenhouse gases include degradation of forests and disposal of wood products, especially paper products, after they have served their period of usefulness.

Figure 5.1 - An aerial view of a brush fire in the Sudan. Roughly 750 million ha of savanna vegetation are burned annually, resulting in a massive release of greenhouse gases.

30. WHAT ARE THE CURRENT RATES OF DEFORESTATION IN THE WORLD'S FORESTS?

The average annual rate of tropical deforestation during the decade of 1981-90 was 15.4 million ha (FAO 1993). These rates of deforestation are roughly equivalent to the total land area of Nepal, Nicaragua or Greece and resulted in a reduction in the area of tropical forests from 1 910 million ha at the end of 1980 to 1 756 million ha at the end of 1990. On a regional basis, the annual loss of forest cover was: Latin America and the Caribbean, 7.4 million ha (0.8% of the total forest area), Asia and the Pacific, 3.9 million ha (1.2 %) and Africa, 4.1 million ha (0.7%). The forest area of the temperate and boreal zones did not change significantly during the same period.

Annual rates of deforestation in the tropics have increased when compared to the previous decade. During the 1980s, the annual rate of tropical deforestation was 11.3 million ha (Lanly 1982).

Forests in developed temperate regions now cover much smaller areas than in the past. These forests have historically contributed heavily to global carbon emissions as forests in Europe and North America were cleared for agriculture. However, the area of these forests has stabilized and even increased slightly over the past 100 years as agricultural lands were abandoned and reverted to forest cover. France, for example, had forest cover on only 14% of the country's land area in 1798. Today 27% of its land area is forested. Deforestation and agricultural development in the state of Vermont, USA had reduced the surface area of forest cover to about 15% of the total land area about 100 years ago. Today the state is 85% forested.

31. HOW ARE FOREST SOILS AFFECTED BY DEFORESTATION?

In addition to increasing susceptibility of soils to erosion by wind and water, the clearing of forests and woodlands to support agriculture in the tropics can result in a loss of 20 to 50% of the soil carbon contained in the topsoil. Some estimates indicate that deforestation in the tropics caused a net release of between 0.1 and 0.3 Gt of soil carbon in the years around 1990 compared with 0.3 and 1.3 Gt as a result of burning and decay of vegetation respectively (Sombroek et al 1993).

Chapter 6
POSSIBLE EFFECTS OF CLIMATE CHANGE ON FORESTS

32. WHAT CHANGES IN GROWTH AND YIELD OF TREES AND FORESTS CAN BE EXPECTED AS A RESULT OF CLIMATE CHANGE?

The implications of CO_2 enrichment on growth and yield of trees and forests are still unclear. Laboratory studies on growth rates and yield of plants grown in elevated CO_2 environments have documented increased rates of photosynthesis, lowered plant water use requirements, increased carbon sequestration and increased soil microbial activity. These result in higher rates of nitrogen fixation, thereby stimulating growth. However in a natural ecosystem, where animals graze on plants, disease organism cause damage and tree death and plants compete for available light, water and nutrients, there are serious doubts that production would actually increase. In addition, higher growth and yield could be offset by higher losses due to fire, insects and disease (See questions 35 and 36).

To date, little work has been done to test the effects of higher CO_2 concentrations on forests or other natural plant communities over extended time frames. Therefore the net effect of climate change on forest growth and yield uncertain. Sedjo and Solomon (1989) conclude that the phenomenon of CO_2 fertilization has not yet been detected in trees, despite extensive searches for it in the field and in growth chambers.

33. *WHAT CHANGES CAN BE EXPECTED IN THE NATURAL RANGES OF TREE SPECIES AND PLANT COMMUNITIES DUE TO CLIMATE CHANGE?*

When temperature and rainfall patterns change, the ranges of both animal and plant species change. As the Earth warms, species tend to shift their distributions toward higher latitudes and altitudes. **For each 1°C of warming, tree ranges in the northern hemisphere have the potential to expand 100 km northward while southern boundaries retreat.** This is a process which has been tracked since the last Ice Age (Davis 1989).

There is ample evidence in the fossil record that plants have undergone significant range shifts in response to changing climates. Analysis of fossil pollen data also provides information on the composition of past vegetation (Brubaker 1975, Solomon and Bartlein 1992) (Fig 6.1). During the Pleistocene interglacial eras, temperatures in North America were from 2° to 3° C higher than they are now. Tree species such as sweetgum, *Liquidambar styraciflua*, and Osage orange, *Maclura pomifera*, which today are considered typical components of forest vegetation in the southeastern United States, occurred near Toronto, Canada. During the last interglacial era, which ended more than 100 000 years ago, areas covered presently with boreal vegetation in northwestern Europe, were predominantly temperate. More recently in Sweden, the range of the birch, *Betula pubescens*, responded rapidly to warming during the first half of the twentieth century by expanding its range northward into the tundra (Peters 1990).

Shifts in the ranges of tree species could be important for several reasons. First, there are indications that climate could change faster than some tree species can respond through migration. Second, new sites may not be edaphically suitable for the migration of species. Finally, future climate zones,

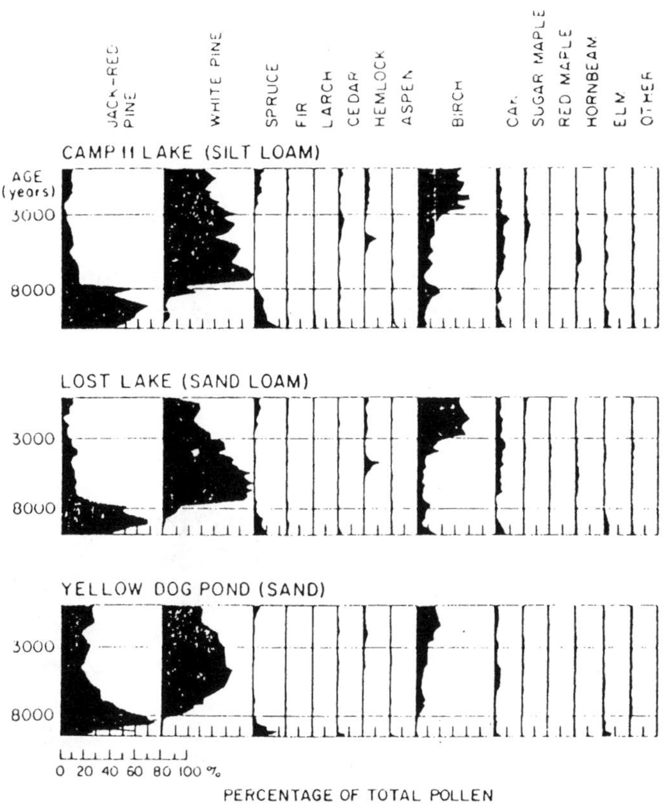

Figure 6.1 - Fossil pollen diagrams made from analysis of lake sediments in the Upper Peninsula of Michigan, USA. These data provide clues as to the composition of forests which occupied this area in the past (Source: Solomon and Bartlein 1992).

leading to displaced forest ecosystems will not be related to current political boundaries and (or) land use patterns (Izrael et al 1990).

Studies have been done which predict shifts in the natural ranges of plant ecosystems (Fig 6.2) and individual tree species which could result from temperature and moisture changes due to atmospheric levels of GHGs. Miller et al

(1987) predict that loblolly pine, *Pinus taeda*, an important industrial forest species in the southeastern USA, would shift approximately 350 km northward in response to a global warming of 3° C (Fig 6.3).

Shifts in the natural ranges of animals and plants will take place in response to the requirements of individual species and not necessarily the ecosystem as a whole. Therefore some re-alignment of species associations can be expected should the climate change.

Species may shift altitudinally as well as latitudinally. As the climate warms, species will shift upwards. Generally a short increase in altitude corresponds to a major shift in latitude (Fig 6.4). For example, a cooling of **3°C associated with a 500 m rise in elevation corresponds to a shift of 250 km in latitude.** Because mountain peaks are smaller than the bases, as species shift upward in response to warming, they typically occupy smaller areas, have smaller populations and may become more vulnerable to genetic and environmental pressures (Peters 1990, Sombroek 1990). This could affect the distribution and abundance of endemic species whose natural ranges are already confined to high elevations in both temperate and tropical ecosystems (e.g. species endemic to high elevation cloud forests in the tropics or the islands of high elevation boreal forests which occur in the southern Appalachian Mountains of the United States).

A recent study by a team of scientists working in the Austrian Alps indicates that alpine plant species are migrating toward mountain summits at rates ranging from less than one meter to nearly four meters per year. This is based on studies undertaken on 26 mountain summits in 1992 and compared with historical surveys of alpine plant species on the same mountains 70-90 years ago. The central Alps have warmed by 0.7°C over the same time period (Grabherr et al 1994).

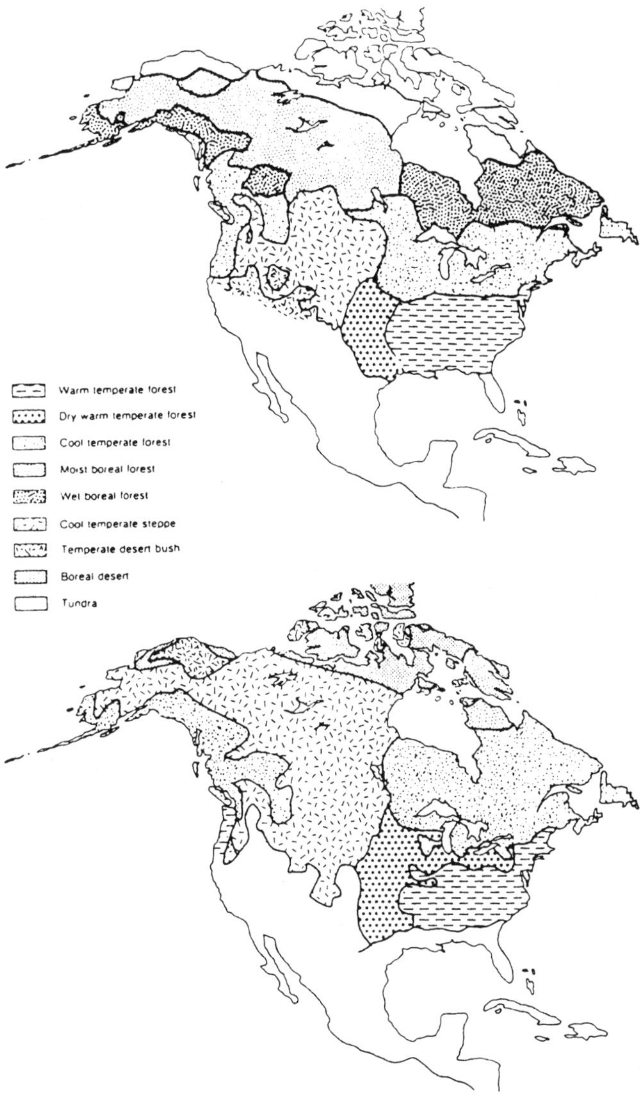

Figure 6.2 - Holdridge Life-Zone Classification of vegetation types for present day (upper) and under a doubled CO_2 scenario of temperature (Source Pollard 1985, redrawn from Parry and Carter 1984).

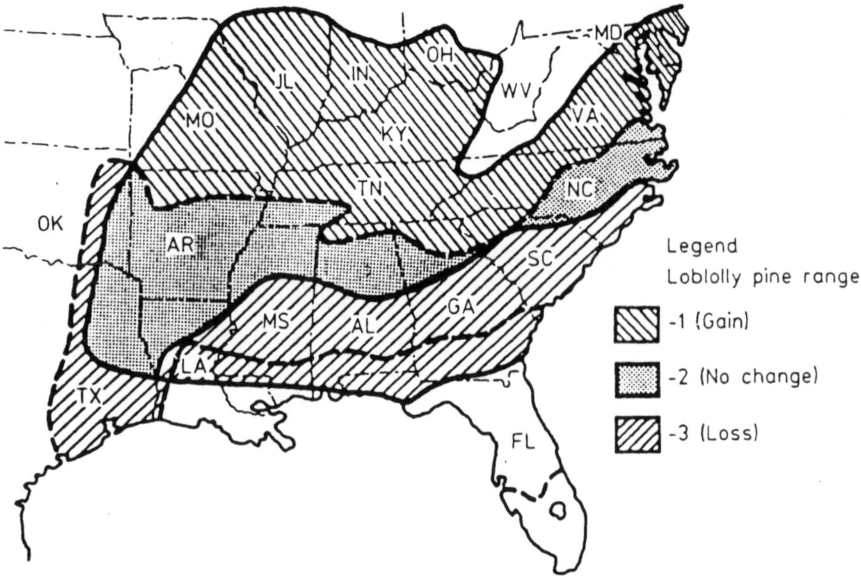

Figure 6.3 - Possible redistribution of loblolly pine, *Pinus taeda* in the southeastern United States due to a doubling of atmospheric CO_2 (Source - Miller et al 1987).

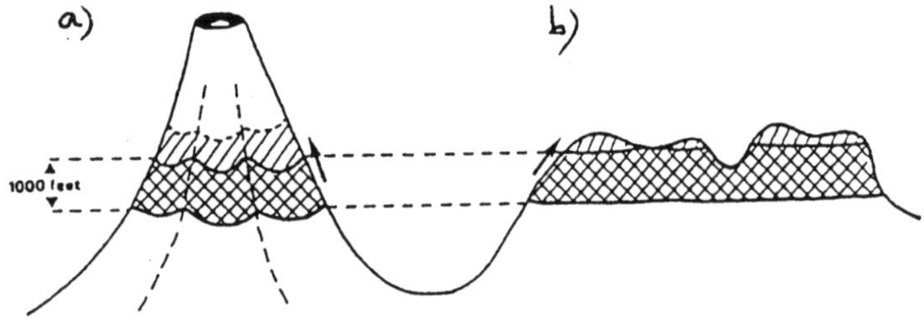

Figure 6.4 - Examples of species redistribution in high mountain regions due to a 2°C increase in mean annual temperature: a = mountains of eastern Africa resulting in a relatively small increase in area and b = highlands of Uganda resulting in a near disappearance of a high elevation vegetation zone (Source: Sombroek 1990).

Box 6.1 Will the future forests of the world be drier?

Plants may have reduced rates of transpiration in an atmosphere with elevated levels of CO_2. The outcome could be a world with reduced cloud formation and less rain, according to a report by the Terrestrial Initiative on Global Environmental Research (TIGER) of the Natural Environmental Research Council of the United Kingdom.

Several research groups have successfully linked computer models of land surface processes to climate prediction models. A simple climate model predicted nearly 10% more evaporation and 3% more rainfall over the tropical rain forests in a future high CO_2 environment. However, when the rainforest was described more realistically, a new chain of events was started, leading to less water being available for cloud formation and less evaporation and rain (WMO 1994).

Sea level rise, associated with rising temperatures, could effect the distribution and abundance of mangrove forests. These coastal forests provide a wealth of wood and non wood forest products and services. In addition to meeting needs for wood products for the inhabitants of coastal zones in the tropics, they provide a rich habitat for fisheries and aquaculture. They also protect coastal zones from tropical storms and shoreline erosion and offer breeding sites for a large number of wildlife species (FAO 1994, Gable et al 1990).

Future shifts in the natural ranges of trees and forest communities could have both positive and negative effects on supplies of lumber and other forest products, distance to markets, species diversity and susceptibility to fire, pests and disease.

34. WHAT IS THE LIKELIHOOD THAT CLIMATE CHANGE COULD THREATEN SOME SPECIES OR PLANT COMMUNITIES WITH EXTINCTION?

The likelihood that plant or animal species could be lost due to climate change is uncertain. Because of their mobility, animals are generally at less risk because they are able to disperse to habitats which are more favourable. Plants, on the other hand, are stationary, and must rely on dispersal of seeds from areas which are no longer favourable to new areas resulting in a gradual shift in the their natural ranges. During the Pleistocene glacial eras many tree species were lost from the boreal and temperate forests of Europe because they were unable to shift their ranges southward due to the presence of the Alps, the Pyrenees and other predominantly east-west mountain ranges which served as a natural barrier to plant migration. Consequently, the forests of northern Europe contain considerably fewer species than those which occur at equivalent latitudes in Asia and North America.

In general, plant ecologists believe that plant species with broad geographic ranges and many populations will be the most likely to survive climate change. Examples include species such as *Pinus sylvestris*, which occurs from western Europe to Siberia, *Populus tremula* and *P. tremuloides*, both of which have transcontinental distributions. Rare or geographically restricted species would be at greater risk of extinction. This is especially true of species restricted to high elevation zones which would ultimately be unable to shift their ranges further upslope in response to a warmer climate. An example is the Fraser or southern balsam fir, *Abies fraseri*, a tree whose natural range is restricted to the highest elevations of six areas in the Southern Appalachian Mountains in the United States (Fig 6.5). Another category of plants which are at some risk of extinction are those with heavy seeds which are not readily dispersed.

Figure 6.5 - A forest of *Abies fraseri* and *Picea rubens* straddles the highest ridges in the Black Mountains of North Carolina, USA. Forests such as these would be unable to shift their ranges upslope in response to a warming climate.

Other ecologists argue that the risk of extinction of plant species and resultant loss of biodiversity is minimal because plants possess genetic variation which allows them to adapt to changing environmental conditions. Genetic variation is a prerequisite for evolution and a powerful mechanism which allows both animals and plants to change and adapt (Eriksson et al 1993).

35. HOW MIGHT CLIMATE CHANGE INFLUENCE THE INCIDENCE AND INTENSITY OF WILDFIRES?

As the structure, composition and biomass of forests respond to changing climate, so will the behaviour of fire (Fosberg et al 1990). Some expected changes include increases in the frequency and severity of fires and a lengthening of fire seasons in areas which are already prone to fire events.

Some tropical rain forests are subject to periodic episodes of prolonged droughts such as those caused by the El Niño Southern Oscillation (ENSO). These droughts can drastically change the fuel conditions and flammability of the vegetation. Once precipitation falls below 100 mm per month, and periods of two or more weeks without rain occur, the forest vegetation sheds its leaves progressively with increasing drought stress. In addition, the moisture content of surface fuels is lowered, while fallen woody material and loosely packed leaf litter contributes to the build-up and spread of surface fires. Aerial fuels such as desiccated climbers and lianas become fire ladders leading to crown fires (Goldammer and Seibert 1990). It is this sequence of events which set the stage for the catastrophic fires which occurred in East Kalimantan, Indonesia during 1982-83 and resulted in the destruction of over 3.5 million ha of primary and secondary moist forest. Some global circulation models (GCM) predict increased drought episodes in some tropical forests. Consequently the incidence of large wildfires, such as the ones which occurred in East Kalimantan, could increase.

Certain tropical rain forests, especially those in the sub-equatorial tropics (from 10 to 23° latitude) are subject to hurricanes. Damage associated with these storms promotes invasion of vines, which can contribute to foliar biomass accumulation on soil surface openings, particularly during occasional dry spells. This results in fuel loadings that can lead to fires (Mueller-Dombois and Goldammer 1990).

Fuel accumulation resulting from the direct effects of tropical storms can also increase the hazard of wildfire. In 1988, Hurricane Gilbert swept across part of Mexico's Yucatan Peninsula and damaged over 1 million ha of tropical forests. The volume of combustible fuel created by the debris increased the risk of wildfire. During the following year, over 120,000 ha of Mexico's largest area of tropical forest burned (Ciesla 1993). One of the more uncertain effects of predicted climate change is the possibility of an increased frequency and intensity of tropical storms. This would increase the levels of combustible fuels.

In some remote forest areas, lightning is a major cause of fire. A study using GCMs was done to determine lightning frequency for a doubled CO_2 climatic regime. This study predicts an increase in lightning frequency at all latitudes with a mean global increase of 26% (Fosberg et al 1990).

36. WHAT ARE THE EXPECTED EFFECTS OF CLIMATE CHANGE ON FOREST HEALTH INCLUDING SUSCEPTIBILITY TO PESTS AND DISEASE OR DECLINE?

An increase in insect and disease caused losses in forests could become one of the first observed effects of climate change. Evidence of this can be found in the pest epidemics which are the result of stress brought on by periodic drought or excess rainfall. Reviews by Kristiansen (1993) and Sauerbeck (1992) of potential effects of climate change on pests and diseases in agriculture provide a framework from which to identify potential forest sector effects. They include both positive and negative responses.

Some anticipated **negative** effects on forest health are:

* In a given location, higher temperatures could result in more generations of insect pests per year, thus increasing their destructive potential. This is especially true for those insects which already have more than one generation a year. An example of a destructive forest insect of tropical forests whose number of generations could increase under a warming scenario is the pine caterpillar, *Dendrolimus punctatus*, an important defoliator of tropical pines in southern China and Southeast Asia (Fig 6.6)

* The ratios of pest species to their natural enemies could change in favour of the pests. This would increase the reproductive potential of destructive pests and result in higher levels of damage.

* Increased climatic anomalies are predicted to occur as part of climate change. A higher incidence of droughts, storms, deep freeze events or periods of excess rainfall will put additional stresses on trees and forests making them more susceptible to attack by pests and disease. Climatic anomalies may also increase the sensitivity of trees to air pollution from anthropogenic sources. Episodes of forest decline may also increase. These are the result of a complex interaction of forests with climate, site, pests and disease and, in many cases, human activities (Mueller-Dombois 1992). Examples include diebacks of *Metrosideros*

Figure 6.6 - Insects such as the pine caterpillar, *Dendrolimus punctatus*, a destructive defoliator of tropical pines in Southeast Asia, can undergo additional generations in warmer climates.

polymorpha in the Hawaiian Islands, USA, *Azadirachta indica* in the Sahel region of Africa, *Acacia nilotica* in the Sudan and *Eucalyptus* spp in Australia and South America (Ciesla and Donaubauer 1994).

* Widening carbon/nitrogen ratios in trees due to elevated levels of CO_2 could increase foliage consumption by insects as has been demonstrated in laboratory studies. For example, Lincoln et al (1984) showed that feeding rates of lepidopterous larvae rose with corresponding increases in atmospheric CO_2. Forest defoliators such as the spruce budworms, *Choristoneura* spp., in North America and pine caterpillars, *Dendrolimus* spp. in Asia could be similarly affected. As a result outbreaks could cause more severe defoliation. More recently Lincoln (1993) showed similar feeding responses from larvae representing another group of foliage feeding insects; pine sawflies, *Neodiprion* sp. (Hymenoptera: Diprionidae).

* A higher incidence of insect and disease outbreaks due to stress on trees associated with climate change will result in higher levels of combustible fuels in forests increasing the risk of wildfires. In the conifer forests of western North America, recent outbreaks of several species of bark beetles (Family Scolytidae) have increased the volumes of flammable fuels to dangerously high levels. These have resulted in large fires of high intensity including the 1988 fire in Yellowstone National Park in the USA. These outbreaks are believed to be related to fire exclusion and not climate change, however they serve as an example of what could happen as a result of

predicted climate change (Hessburg et al 1994, USDA 1994)

Some possible **positive** effects are:

* The higher growth rates which are projected by some scientists, due to warmer temperatures and elevated CO_2 levels might allow forests to sustain higher levels of insect and disease damage without reductions in growth and yield.

* The increased vigour of trees and forests growing in elevated CO_2 levels could be more resistant to attack by insects and disease.

* Elevated CO_2 may benefit plant health and productivity by altering the morphology and physiology of plants to the detriment of disease causing organisms.

The hazard of destructive insect and disease outbreaks in tropical forests is believed to be minimal when compared to temperate and boreal forests because of their inherent diversity. While this may be true in tropical forests of natural origin, it must be kept in mind that many tropical countries, to meet their needs for wood products, rely on single species plantations, often of fast growing exotics. Many of these plantations are established with material representing a narrow genetic base. These are often unable to adapt to changing environmental conditions. In 1990, there were an estimated 30.7 million ha of forest plantations in 90 tropical countries (FAO 1993). A total of 23% were of *Eucalyptus* spp and 10% were of various species of *Pinus*. These are subject to attack by a variety of pests, many of which are accidentally introduced. An excellent review of forest insect and disease plantation pests of the Asia-Pacific Region is provided by Hutacharern et al (1990). This review clearly indicates that in tropical managed forests, there is an ample number of insect and disease pests which could respond to changes in climate.

Box 6.2. **Dieback of *Juniperus procera* in Kenya - an example of the effects of a regional climate change?**

Dieback and mortality of *Juniperus procera*, an important component of highland forests in Kenya has been occurring at least since the early 1980's. In some places, up to 90% of the trees have been affected. The heaviest dieback and mortality occurs in the drier low elevation forests. Higher elevation stands, which receive more precipitation and grow on better soils appear to be in a reasonably good state of health.

The factors responsible for this condition are unknown. One hypothesis is that these forests have been stressed by a long term regional warming and drying trend which has affected the low elevation sites to the point where they are no longer suitable for this species (Ciesla et al 1994). As a result, the altitudinal range of this species could become more restricted in the future.

Chapter 7
HELPING FORESTS ADAPT TO CLIMATE CHANGE

37. HOW CAN WE RESPOND TO PREDICTED CLIMATE CHANGE?

There are two overall approaches to responding to predicted climate change; **adaptation** and **mitigation**. These approaches apply to all sectors involved in the climate change issue.

ADAPTATION is concerned with responses to the **effects** of climate change. It refers to any adjustment, whether passive, reactive or anticipatory that can be adopted to ameliorate the anticipated expected or actual adverse consequences effects of climate change. Adaptation also includes taking advantage of any possible beneficial effects such as longer growing seasons which might allow planting of certain crops at higher latitudes.

Many adaptation policies make good sense regardless of climate change because present day climatic variability and extreme climatic events, such as droughts, severe storms and floods already cause significant damage in most parts of the world. Adaptation to these events can help reduce damage in the short term regardless of any long term changes in climate.

MITIGATION or "limitation" attempts to address the **causes** of climate change. It achieves this through actions which prevent or retard increases in levels of atmospheric GHGs by limiting current and future emission sources and enhancing potential sinks of GHGs.

Both adaptation and mitigation strategies should be considered in an integrated approach when designing responses to climate change. This chapter addresses opportunities for helping forests adapt to climate change while Chapter 8 addresses mitigation options.

38. DO NATURAL PROCESSES EXIST WHICH CAN HELP TREES AND FORESTS ADAPT TO A CHANGING CLIMATE?

Some populations of trees, because of their genetic variability, will be able to survive the effects of climate change by adjusting to the new conditions through acclimation rather than by migrating to new locations with climates similar to the original habitat. Another potential adaptive mechanism is that certain physiological and developmental traits will undergo permanent changes as a result of evolution.

In many cases, the boundaries of a species' range may be a consequence of factors operating in addition to climate. One of these factors is competition. In the northern hemisphere, the southern limits or lower elevation limits of the ranges of many species are determined by competitive relationships with species to the south or at lower elevations. Thus, many northern species grow quite well in non-competitive situations far south of their natural ranges. If climate changes, these species may be able to persist in their original locations if the better competitors do not invade immediately.

Often, reproduction and seedling establishment is more sensitive to climate change than is the survival of mature individuals. In such cases, adult individuals may persist in an area long after regeneration has disappeared.

39. HOW CAN FOREST MANAGEMENT HELP FORESTS ADAPT TO CLIMATE CHANGE?

Good silvicultural practices, including maintenance of optimum stocking levels and selection of trees which are best adapted to existing sites should ensure that forests remain vigorous and relatively free of site and stand related stress. These practices should help forests adapt to climate change.

Practices which could help forests adapt to a changing climate include:

* Shorter rotation lengths which would reduce the probability of senescence related stresses and related hazard of damage by pests and disease.
* Control of competition for available moisture, light and soil nutrients.
* Selection of species and provenances best adapted to existing site conditions.
* Properly scheduled thinning to maximize growth and increase resistance to damage from high winds, insects and disease.
* Tree improvement programmes to create planting stock from a broad genetic base with high growth rates, better form and adaptability to a wide range of site conditions.
* Protection from the destructive effects of fire, pests and disease (see questions 35 and 36).
* Periodic inventories and stand examinations to provide the basis for silvicultural prescriptions and harvest scheduling.

40. WHAT CAN BE DONE TO HELP FORESTS ADAPT TO INCREASED HAZARDS OF WILDFIRE AND (OR) PEST AND DISEASE OUTBREAKS WHICH COULD RESULT FROM CLIMATE CHANGE?

Regardless of climate change considerations, forest health management should be an integral part of *all* forest management activities. In the future, however, it will be even more necessary to consider potential effects of climate change on fire, insects and diseases in the development of strategic forest sector development plans including those funded through international assistance activities such as the Tropical Forests Action Programme (TFAP).

Programmes designed to protect the health of forests should include a monitoring component, decision criteria for the management of fire, pests and disease based on sound ecological, economic and social criteria, and a number of environmentally friendly tactics (biological, chemical, cultural, mechanical and regulatory) which can be used in modern forest fire management and integrated pest management (IPM) systems to create conditions unfavourable for the development of major fire events or outbreaks of pests and disease and to provide for an effective response to these events.

Some strategies and tactics to consider in the integration of climate change into the development of forest fire, insect and disease management programmes include:

* Increase the capacity of developing countries to provide leadership to modern forest fire management programmes including prevention, presuppression planning and suppression and to improve forest health through silviculture and integrated pest management.

* Place greater emphasis on matching tree species and provenances to sites in tree planting programmes. Avoid use of planting stock from a narrow genetic base which may not have the inherent resilience to adapt to changing climatic conditions.

* Reduce reliance on one or two tree species in afforestation and reforestation programmes. Instead, include a number of species, where

feasible in mixed species plantings, which are well adapted to local sites and climatic conditions and meet national needs for forest products and services.

* Establish *in-situ* and *ex-situ* reserves of key forest species to ensure that a gene pool of sufficient variability is available for tree improvement programmes which have the objective of developing varieties capable of adapting to climate change.

* Accelerate timber salvage and fuel management programmes to reduce the hazard of wildfire in forests, especially those which have suffered from high levels of pest and disease damage or forest decline events.

* Design insect and disease monitoring programmes which are capable of detecting increases in the occurrence and intensity of forest decline events and in the activity of new pests and diseases (both indigenous and introduced) in addition to those which have historically caused losses. Monitoring systems should also be capable of detecting changes in the biology, ecology and natural ranges of pest species including timing of key events in their life histories, number of generations, feeding patterns and pest/host interactions.

* Initiate research programmes to determine effects of long term climate change on the biology and pest-disease/host interactions of traditional pest species. In addition, identify those species which have a potential for becoming pests under a climate change

scenario. Integrate new research information into operating programmes as soon as possible.

* Conduct studies on the effects of fire, insects and disease on biodiversity in terms of colonizers, successional and climax species. Determine the degree of "disruptions" in the self repairing process of vegetation systems due to climate change. Examples include the inability of forests to re-invade burned or harvested areas, or an "arrested" succession, where scrub or liana vegetation is no longer replaced by forest.

* Initiate studies to determine the effects of climatic anomalies on forest stability.

CHAPTER 8
THE ROLE OF FORESTS AND FORESTRY FOR MITIGATING THE EFFECTS OF CLIMATE CHANGE

41. WHAT OPPORTUNITIES DO FORESTS AND FOREST MANAGEMENT OFFER FOR MITIGATING THE EFFECTS OF PREDICTED CLIMATE CHANGE?

Forests provide opportunities to partially mitigate the predicted effects of climate change. This can be accomplished through three overall approaches:

Reducing sources of greenhouse gases.

Maintaining existing sinks of greenhouse gases.

Expanding sinks of greenhouse gases.

Specific actions under each of these approaches are described in sections 8A - 8C of this chapter.

Two things must be kept in mind when planning forest sector strategies and programmes designed to mitigate effects of climate change:

* Trees and forests are only **temporary** carbon sinks. When trees are harvested, burned or die, some of the stored carbon is again released into the atmosphere. Forest sector policies and strategies therefore should aim at **prolonging** the carbon storage capacity of trees and forests as long as possible.

* Any forest sector mitigation measures must be done in concert with mitigation measures in **other sectors** that contribute significantly to the build up of GHGs in the atmosphere such as industry, agriculture, transportation and power generation.

42. WHAT FEATURES SHOULD CHARACTERIZE ACTIONS TAKEN TO MITIGATE POTENTIAL EFFECTS OF CLIMATE CHANGE?

Regardless of what actions are taken to mitigate the predicted affects of climate change, they should have the following characteristics:

Ecologically Sustainable - Actions should provide for the long term needs of both present and future generations.

Economically Viable - Proposed actions should have low start up costs and be socially integrative, building on local needs, life styles and traditions.

Technologically Simple - Actions should be capable of being implemented successfully under a variety of conditions with a minimum of specialized equipment, training or procedures.

Adaptable - They should have sufficient flexibility to adapt to changing economic, political, social, ecological and climatic conditions.

Socially Acceptable - Proposed actions should have immediate and clear benefits, especially to local residents.

43. WHAT ADDITIONAL RESEARCH IS NEEDED TO MORE FULLY UNDERSTAND THE POTENTIAL EFFECTS OF CLIMATE CHANGE ON TREES AND FORESTS AND TO DEVELOP ADAPTATION AND MITIGATION TACTICS?

There are many uncertainties associated with all aspects of the global climate change issue. With regard to forests and forestry there are uncertainties concerning the impact of possible climate change on forest ecosystems, the adaptation of forests to climate change and the potential for mitigating predicted adverse effects of climate change by forests.

During a Ministerial Conference on the Protection of Forests in Europe held in Helsinki, Finland in 1993, the European states and the European Union agreed to a programme of intensified research and cooperation on forestry and climate change. This programme provides a comprehensive model for national and (or) regional efforts and recommends the following lines of investigation:

* Achieve a greater understanding of the linkages between climate change and forest ecosystems, including feed-backs from ecosystems to the climate system.

* Quantify the role of forests, forest soils and peatlands as reservoirs, sinks and sources of carbon and understand the role of forests in the global carbon cycle. Research in this field may include the development of common methodologies for research, for national and regional inventories and the development and maintenance of data bases on reservoirs, sinks and sources of carbon in terrestrial ecosystems.

* Identify the genetic variability associated with regionally important tree species and their ability to respond to changes in climate and increased concentration of carbon dioxide, and on the degree and rate of evolutionary processes and adaptation.

* Determine the dynamic equilibrium of host-parasite relationships in new climatic environments.

* Study changes in soil formation processes, including the mineralisation of organic matter and leaching, in response to climate change.

* Develop process-based predictive ecosystem models applicable on a regional scale which may be used in to integrate anticipated changes in climate, interactions with air pollution, effects on forest ecosystems, fluxes of greenhouse gases and effects on forests and forest management.

* Define ways to alter forest management systems to optimise adaptation to climate change, ensure the health and functions of forests and to optimise the sequestration and storage of carbon.

A conceptual plan for research in forest/atmospheric interactions in the United States has also been designed by USDA Forest Service (USDA 1988).

44. DO INTERNATIONAL AGREEMENTS EXIST WHICH ENCOURAGE DEVELOPMENT AND PROTECTION OF FORESTS TO ENHANCE THEIR ABILITY TO MITIGATE THE EFFECTS OF CLIMATE CHANGE?

Several international instruments and targets have been developed which support large scale forest sector development as a means of mitigating the effects of predicted climate change.

One of the first international accords on climate change which referred directly to forestry was the Nordwijk Declaration on Climate Change which was developed in 1989. This declaration established a target of a net growth in forest area of 12 million ha/yr by the beginning of the next century. A follow up workshop held in Bangkok, Thailand in 1991 concluded that the prospect for attaining such a target was very limited (IPCC 1992).

During the United Nations Conference on Environment and Development (UNCED), held in Rio de Janiero, Brazil, a Framework Convention on Climate Change, designed to control and reduce future GHG emissions was signed. This convention was ratified by 100 signatory countries by December 1994.

A non-legally binding authoritative statement entitled "Principles for a Global Consensus on the Management, Conservation and Sustainable Development of all Types of Forests" was adopted at the UNCED conference. The statement stresses that forest lands should be sustainably managed to meet the social, economic, ecological, cultural and spiritual human needs of present and future generations. These principles and Agenda 21, an environmental programme for the 21st century which was also promulgated at UNCED, propose forest conservation measures to conserve carbon pools and increase the security of these pools.

These statements which must be translated into action programmes at the country and community level in order to be implemented. Several countries, including China, Denmark, Finland, France and Italy have developed strategic action plans under the umbrella of these international agreements. France, for example, has targeted the addition of 30 000 ha of afforestation annually for the next 50 years and the promotion of more durable uses of wood (e.g. in construction) (Ministère de l'Agriculture et de la Pêche 1994).

International agencies, such as FAO, can provide a wide range of technical assistance and training related to climate change and identification of opportunities for forests to mitigate its effects.

45. *HOW CAN THE TROPICAL FORESTS ACTION PROGRAMME (TFAP) ASSIST IN DEVELOPING FOREST SECTOR PROGRAMMES TO HELP MITIGATE EFFECTS OF CLIMATE CHANGE?*

TFAP is designed to assist countries in the conservation and sustainable use of tropical forest resources. The plan grew out of parallel efforts sponsored by FAO, The World Bank (WB), the United Nations Development Programme (UNDP) and the World Resources Institute (WRI). The Programme was formalized in 1987 and strengthened in 1991. Leadership for the programme is housed in FAO.

TFAP is a country-driven approach to forest resource planning and management. The process involves a high level of participation by local people and non-government organisations, is multidisciplinary and intersectorial. TFAP begins with the formulation or revision of a long term forest policy and strategy and the development of a national forest plan. This process can facilitate the integration of climate change considerations into the development and implementation of long range forest sector policies, strategies and plans.

8A
REDUCING SOURCES OF GREENHOUSE GASES

46. WHAT ACTIONS CAN BE TAKEN TO REDUCE THE CURRENT RATES OF TROPICAL DEFORESTATION AND HOW MIGHT THIS AFFECT EMISSIONS OF GHGS FROM FORESTS?

Arresting the current rates of deforestation requires actions which **reduce pressures** to convert forest lands to other uses and to **protect** remaining forests so that they can be managed on a sustainable basis. Most deforestation is caused by the expansion of agriculture. This is in direct response to expanding human populations and economic development. Programmes aimed at reducing deforestation must, therefore, be accompanied by efforts to increase productivity and sustainability of existing agricultural lands so that production keeps pace with increasing demands. In many cases, deforestation has been considered as being only a forest sector problem when in reality it is a multisectoral issue.

Acccrding to one estimate, as much as 80% of forest clearing for shifting and sedentary agriculture can be eliminated by substituting sustainable cropping systems (Lashof and Tirpak (1989). They suggest the following actions for reducing the expansion of agriculture into tropical forests:

* Introduce crop mixes, planting and management systems and improved genetic strains of crops to increase productivity per unit area on existing agricultural lands. In some cases, investment in fertilizers, irrigation systems and capital (high input systems) will be needed to achieve adequate agricultural intensification and sustainability.

* Conduct research on use of low external input cropping systems where high inputs are not feasible.

* Develop opportunities for raising of cash crops as well as subsistence crops so that farmers can acquire needed cash to invest in fertilizers, irrigation equipment and other technologies.

* Intensify management of existing pasture lands to increase site productivity through the introduction of optimized foraging strategies, fertilization, mechanisation and improved livestock management.

* Focus agricultural development on sites with adequate non-forest soils such as savannah, pasture and under-utilised crop lands.

The opportunities for implementing these and other options should be determined through the development of strategic land and resource management plans at the national level.

47. WHAT CAN BE DONE TO REDUCE THE FREQUENCY AND SCALE OF FORESTS AND SAVANNA WOODLAND CONSUMED BY BIOMASS BURNING?

Most fires which occur in the savannas and woodlands of the tropics are **prescribed** or intentional fires. These are set by local residents who use fire to clear land, dispose of agricultural residues, improve the quality of forage for livestock or to drive game animals. These practices are based on traditions which are often thousands of years old. Unless there are massive changes in agricultural and range management practices in these countries in the near future, these practices and resultant carbon emissions will continue in the future.

Prescribed fires often escape and burn over areas which are not intended to be burned. The number and area burned by **wildfires** or unintentional fires can be reduced through implementation of **integrated** fire management programmes. While the primary benefit of these programmes is the protection of forest and other wildland resources from wildfire, they will also reduce carbon emissions.

The elements of an integrated wildfire management programme include fire **prevention, presuppression planning** (fire detection, fire danger rating based on local fire weather and fuel conditions (Fig 8.1), training and equipping of fire brigades) and **suppression**, the actual fighting of forest and woodland fires.

Prevention should be directed toward specific groups of people which cause wildfires. For example, in Indonesia, woodlands in several national parks are under a high risk of wildfire because of agricultural burning by neighbouring farmers. This was one of the target groups identified as part of a project funded through the FAO Technical Cooperation Programme (TCP) in wildfire management. The subsequent fire prevention programme specifically addressed this group. Another key aspect of prevention is fuels management. This includes establishment of fuel breaks in strategic locations and periodic use of prescribed burning to reduce volumes of combustible fuels. A relatively simple procedure such as teaching farmers how to construct fire breaks around pastures or fields which are to be burned can prevent prescribed fires from escaping and burning surrounding forests and woodlands.

When designing wildfire management programmes, it is necessary to have an understanding of the ecological role of natural fires in the areas which are to be protected. In many semi-arid ecosystems, fire plays a key role in plant succession. Fire exclusion can result in the establishment of more vegetative biomass than the site is capable of carrying. This

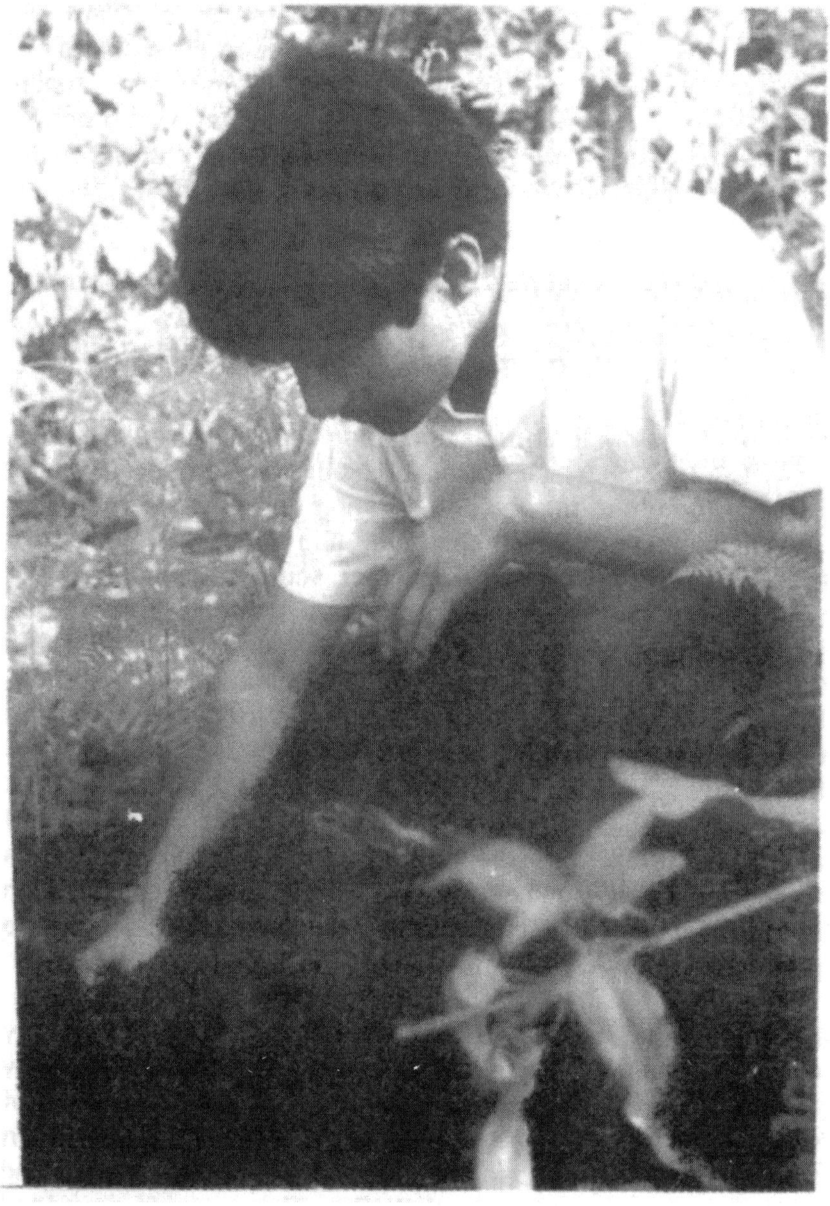

Figure 8.1 - A forester in Mexico's Yucatan Peninsula assesses forest fuels. Knowledge of fuel conditions is an important factor in planning forest fire management programmes.

vegetation subsequently becomes susceptible to attack by insects, disease and other damaging agents resulting in excessively high accumulations of combustible fuels. Consequently, when a wildfire does occur after a long period of fire exclusion, it burns with greater intensity and can be more damaging (Hessburg et al 1994, USDA 1994).

48. HOW CAN INCREASING THE EFFICIENCY OF BURNING FUEL WOOD AND OTHER BIOFUELS REDUCE EMISSIONS OF GHGS?

Fuelwood and other biofuels, including charcoal, crop residues, animal dung and other forms of biomass are used in many parts of the world for cooking, heating and processing of raw materials at the household level (Fig 8.2). Biofuels are presently the fourth most important source of energy in the world with fuelwood and charcoal consumption alone accounting for 10% of overall world energy consumption. In developing countries, biomass is the dominant energy source. For example, in Ethiopia, biofuels account for over 93% of the national energy supply (Karekezi 1994). Use of household biofuels is estimated to contribute between 2 and 7% of the annual emissions of GHGs from human sources. Fuelwood and other biofuels are also used in many developing countries to support many small and medium scale rural industries such as charcoal kilns, bakery ovens, brick kilns, tobacco and coffee processing plants.

In most cases, household biofuels are converted into energy using methods which are inefficient and produce a low energy output. They also produce a high GHG output per unit of energy produced. The use of more efficient combustion systems provides an opportunity to **increase** energy output and **reduce** the per unit output of GHGs. They provide an added benefit of reduced pressure on existing biofuel resources. This is especially important in many semi-arid regions where rapidly

Figure 8.2 - Fuelwood is taken from a forest plantation to a village in Indonesia. Rural people in developing countries rely heavily on fuelwood for cooking and heating. More efficient use of biofuels offers another opportunity to reduce GHG emissions.

expanding populations are putting increased pressure on biofuel resources, leading to deforestation and desertification.

The introduction of more efficient cooking stoves and industrial processes could reduce fuelwood requirements by 25-70% at a low investment cost. This can also contribute to reduced GHG emissions. In addition, the use of better quality biomass in terms of size, moisture content and heating value, if available, can contribute to heating efficiencies and reduced GHG output. In order to achieve maximum benefits from more energy efficient technologies, their introduction must be accompanied by adequate training in their use such as programmes which are offered by NGO's such as the Foundation for Woodstove Dissemination.

49. HOW CAN USE OF WOOD AND OTHER "BIOFUELS" IN PLACE OF FOSSIL FUELS HELP REDUCE LEVELS OF GHGS IN THE ATMOSPHERE?

The substitution of biomass in place of fossil fuels as a modern energy source has the potential to dramatically change the global warming implications of rising energy consumption, especially in tropical countries. Opportunities exist to use large quantities of agricultural and forest residues that would otherwise go to waste. There are also opportunities to develop biomass crops primarily for energy production. If produced efficiently, "biofuels" could supply a significant proportion of commercial energy demand in coming decades.

The benefits of bioenergy utilization go beyond substitution of fuel sources. Biofuels can not only help to close the CO_2 cycle and reduce GHG emissions, but biomass plantations, established on presently fallow lands, would also expand carbon reservoirs. In addition, the substitution of domestically produced biomass could also contribute to improve the balance of payments of energy poor countries. Other benefits include new job opportunities in rural areas and a decentralization of energy resources.

The most obvious opportunities for use of biomass for energy involve agricultural and industrial wastes. In Indonesia, for example, large quantities of wood wastes from logging and wood processing operations are piled and burned, used for landfill or dumped into rivers and the ocean. These materials are presently considered to be a waste disposal problem rather than a source of energy. It is estimated that in Indonesia, wood wastes from sawmills and plywood plants would be sufficient to produce 1 000 megawatts of electricity. This is equivalent to 20-30% of the energy presently derived from fossil fuels. Sugar cane and rice wastes offer similar opportunities. Some agricultural and industrial wastes can also be incorporated into the soil to increase carbon storage.

The potential for biomass utilization goes beyond the use of waste products. Tropical forestry plantations have recorded yields equivalent to more than 15 tons of carbon per ha per year. Even assuming modest growth rates, these plantations could make a significant contribution to both energy supplies and temporary carbon storage if established over large areas (Trexler et al 1992).

50. HOW CAN MORE EFFICIENT TIMBER HARVESTING REDUCE GHG EMISSIONS FROM FORESTS?

Uncontrolled timber harvesting operations result in excessive soil disturbance, logging residues and damaged residual trees. This causes increased emissions of CO_2 and other GHGs and decreases the capacity of the residual forest to sequester carbon (Pinard 1994). Timber harvesting is a damaging process, no matter how well planned and carefully implemented. However there are certain planning and operational practices which can be implemented to reduce the disruption of forest processes.

Good timber harvesting begins with the development of forest management and harvest plans. The forest management plan includes maps and descriptions of areas to be harvested, areas to be protected, contractual information and other general policies. Harvest plans describe in detail the harvesting operation.

Many of the reductions in logging damage which are characteristic of well managed forests are the results of careful harvest planning (Dykstra and Heinrich 1992). These environmental benefits are generally not expensive and may actually increase the efficiency of the harvesting operation and reduce costs.

Several procedures can significantly reduce logging damage. Pre-felling of vines is often recommended where they bind trees together to reduce felling damage. Directional felling is recommended in areas which are to be selectively logged. This will reduce damage to potential future crop trees and facilitate skidding. Yarding also deserves a great deal of consideration because it can cause damage to soils and residual trees. Exposed soils are subject to erosion and leaching of organic matter including carbon. Yarding damage can be reduced by restricting bulldozers to designated skid trails and maximizing log winching distances. Soil damage can be further minimized by use of yarding systems which move logs suspended in the air (eg skylines, helicopters and balloons).

Increased utilization of felled trees will result in a reduction of overall land area which needs to be logged. A study by FAO (Dykstra 1994) revealed that in several tropical countries, less than 50% of the wood in the main stems of tropical trees felled for harvest is actually utilized. The remainder of the main stem and the other parts of the tree are left in the forest as logging residues. By comparison, the average fraction of the main stems utilized in industrial countries is more than 78%.

Post harvest practices such as removal of stream crossings which impede water flow, proper slash disposal and treatments to promote vegetation growth in denuded areas will help promote recovery of harvested areas (Putz 1994).

An example of the benefits of improved timber harvesting techniques comes from a study done in dipterocarp forests in Sabah, Malaysia (Pinard 1994). Normally, trees over 60 cm in diameter at breast height (dbh) are harvested and skidded to landings by bulldozers. Approximately 8 to 15 trees per ha are removed in this manner and up to 75% of the residual trees suffer logging damage. Prior to logging, these forests can store up to 330 tC/ha. The harvesting operation removes about 80 tC/ha. Through the use of controlled harvesting techniques, it has been demonstrated that if damage to the residual stand can be reduced from 40% to 20%, the additional amount of carbon remaining in the residual forest after 10 years could be over 65 tons/ha (Fig 8.3).

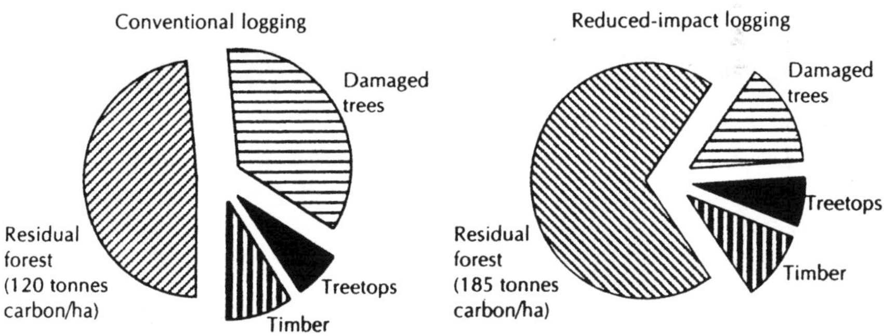

Figure 8.3 - A comparison of residual carbon storage between conventional and reduced impact logging in Malaysia (Source: Pinard 1994)

8B
MAINTAINING EXISTING SINKS OF GREENHOUSE GASES

51. HOW CAN MANAGEMENT AND CONSERVATION OF NATURAL FORESTS ENHANCE THEIR CAPACITY TO FIX AND STORE CARBON?

Improved management of natural forests can increase productivity and carbon storage potential through accelerated growth, maintenance of optimum levels of stocking and protection from fire, pests and disease (See question 40). There are many opportunities worldwide, to improve the management of natural forests. In the tropics, for example, an estimated 137 million ha of logged forests could benefit from enrichment planting and regeneration because present selective logging practices have reduced long term productivity (Grainger 1989) (See question 50).

The development and expansion of non-wood forest products would provide increased incentives to maintain and protect forests. This could have the added desirable effect of increased carbon storage. Examples of opportunities to develop non-wood forest products include production of latex, nuts, resin, mushrooms, wild meat and plants of medicinal value (Fig 8.4).

Establishment of reserved or protected forests, which are excluded from timber harvesting will also help maintain existing natural forests as carbon sinks, provided that they are protected from damaging effects of fire, pests and disease. These forests still provide many opportunities for management of non-timber forest resources. These include providing habitat for wildlife, establishment of sites where rare or endangered plant species can be protected, *in situ*

Figure 8.4 - In Vietnam, a woman collects resin in a pine plantation. Non-wood forest products can provide economic incentives to manage and protect forests, thus maintaining their capacity to absorb and store carbon.

conservation of genetic resources, development of outdoor recreation opportunities, protection of soil and water resources and gathering of non-wood products such as wild fruits and mushrooms. Such forests would probably provide a limited carbon absorption potential however because they often contain large areas of mature forests where carbon absorption is roughly equal to carbon release.

52. WHAT USES OF FORESTS AND FOREST PRODUCTS ARE MOST DESIRABLE FROM THE STANDPOINT OF LONG TERM CARBON STORAGE?

From the perspective of CO_2 storage, the most desirable uses of forest and forest products are those which extend rotation ages and production of goods which are durable and long lasting. This will allow for the carbon to be stored in the woody tissue for as long as possible. However local and national needs for goods and services will prevail over global concerns for carbon sequestration. Therefore, from the socio-economic standpoint, forests should be put to whatever uses are required to support national and local needs, provided that these uses are sustainable. If forests provide for the needs of people, then there are built in incentives to manage them on a sustainable basis and their probability of long term survival and benefit is increased.

Conversion of trees into durable products such as furniture or wooden structures will extend their carbon sequestration. Recycling of paper products will reduce the need for harvesting trees for manufacture into new paper products.

8C
EXPANDING SINKS OF GREENHOUSE GASES

53. HOW MUCH CARBON CAN BE FIXED IN WOOD AND SOIL ON A PER HECTARE BASIS IN FOREST PLANTATIONS IN BOREAL, TEMPERATE AND TROPICAL ZONES?

The rate of carbon fixing is a function of many variables. These include tree species, growth rates, longevity, site, annual precipitation, length of growing season, rotation length, etc. Annual rate of carbon fixing is highest in young plantations.

Fixation rates for several tropical forest plantation species over a given rotation are summarized by Schroeder (1991) (Table 8.1).

TABLE 8.1

CARBON FIXATION RATES FOR SEVERAL TROPICAL FOREST PLANTATION SPECIES
(Source: Schroeder 1991)

Species	Rotation (Yrs)	Mean Above Ground Carbon Storage (Tonnes C/ha)
Pinus caribea	15	59
Leucaena sp.	7-8	21-42
Casuarina sp.	10	21-55
Pinus patula	20	72
Cupressus lusitanica	20	57
Acacia nilotica	10-15	12-17

An overriding factor in afforestation or reforestation is to match the tree species, and provenance to the site on which it is to be planted. In addition, species should be selected which meet the objectives of the plantation and are acceptable to the people of the locality. If these conditions are met, and with proper management and protection, the plantations should be assured of high rates of survival, good growth and will meet the objectives for which they are planted, including sequestration of carbon (Fig 8.5).

54. HOW MUCH ADDITIONAL AREA OF FOREST PLANTATIONS WOULD BE REQUIRED TO FULLY OFFSET PRESENT ANNUAL INCREASES IN GREENHOUSE GAS LEVELS FROM ALL SOURCES?

A number of studies have been conducted to estimate forest area required to offset various CO_2 emission goals. A study by Sedjo and Solomon (1989) indicates that the current annual increase in atmospheric carbon could be sequestered for about 30 years in approximately 465 million ha of plantation forests. This would require an increase of more than 10% in the current area of forests on the earth's surface. It would also represent an increase of more than four times the present plantation area in the world. This estimate is based on the assumption of an average annual growth of 15 m^3/ha/yr. An annual growth rate of 5 m^3/ha/yr is more realistic for plantations in the boreal and temperate zones and for many tropical areas. Therefore this estimate may be highly conservative.

Calculations are presented by Grainger (1990) for several afforestation scenarios. These suggest the following:

* Planting 60 million ha per year for 10 years would establish sufficient forest area to absorb 2.9 GtC per year, the net increment of CO_2 from all sources.

Figure 8.5 - Plantations of fast growing trees, such as this plantation of *Pinus radiata* in Chile, can absorb atmospheric CO_2 while providing a wide range of wood and non-wood products and services.

* Planting 20 million ha per year beginning in 1990 would achieve a carbon absorption equal to the current net annual CO_2 contribution by the year 2020.

* Planting 2 million ha per year for 30 years would establish a forest that could absorb 10% of the net annual increment of CO_2.

* Continuing the present rate of forest planting for the next 40 years will offset less than 10% of the current net CO_2 increase.

* Afforestation of 2 to 5 million ha per year could offset the CO_2 emissions from tropical forests by the year 2020.

The current rate of forest planting in the tropics is about 1.8 million ha per year (FAO 1993).

55. TO WHAT EXTENT ARE SUITABLE LANDS AVAILABLE FOR AFFORESTATION AND REFORESTATION? WHERE ARE THEY?

In order to answer this question, the word "suitable" must first be qualified. It refers not just to a technical definition in terms of soils and climatic conditions. It also depends on social and economic factors. It is possible, at a price, to establish trees almost anywhere; the cost, however, will be not only in money but in human terms, since much of the land that is classified as "degraded" and available for plantations is in fact used by landless people. The decision to commit land area to forest plantations must be technically sound, economically feasible and socially acceptable.

Several estimates of land available for afforestation in the tropics have been made. Grainger (1990) estimates that there may be 621 million ha of land "technically" available. This estimate does not take into account socio-economic considerations. Of this, 418 million ha are in dry, montane regions and 203 million ha are forest fallow in humid areas. According to Houghton (1990), up to 865 million ha of land are available in the tropics for afforestation. Of this total, there may be about 500 million ha of abandoned lands that previously supported forests in Latin America (100 million ha), Asia (100 million ha) and Africa (300 million ha). The additional area would be available only if increases in agricultural productivity on other lands allowed these marginal lands to be removed from production. Winjum et al (1992) estimate that a combination of afforestation, agroforestry and forest protection on 300-600 million ha of available land could conserve and sequester 36-71 Pg C over 50 years.

In the mid and northern latitudes, land uses have stabilized in most areas over the past century, however there are still ample opportunities for re/afforestation projects. In some temperate zone countries, area of forest land has actually increased as marginal agricultural lands which have been abandoned have reverted to natural forests or have been reforested. France was 14% forested in 1789 and today 27% of its land area is forested. Within the past 15 years approximately 600 000 ha *per year* have come out of agricultural production in Europe, of which about 40% was transferred to forest and other wooded land (FAO 1992).

In the United States, there are an estimated 46.8 million ha of crop and pasture lands which are capable of growing trees and are better suited to this purpose. There are also opportunities for planting of fast growing trees for wood energy production on 14-28 million ha and establishment of windbreak plantings on 1.37 million ha. If planted, these areas could provide an additional carbon storage capacity of from 66-210 million tonnes/yr (Sampson and Hamilton 1992).

One type of degraded land that may have potential for the establishment of plantations is salt-affected land, provided it is not used by people who have no other source of land. Reliable and recent estimates of such land are not available but in the tropics there may be over 50 million ha both in Africa and in Asia and over 30 million ha in Latin America as well as large areas in Australia and temperate and sub-tropical Asia (Massoud 1977). There are several active research programmes into the selection of salt-tolerant species and provenances of plantation trees, particularly in Australia and Asia, but it should be noted that there are also research programmes into the development of salt-tolerant agricultural crops. Nevertheless salt-affected soils are an important if unquantified source of land for plantations.

Based on the above information, it would appear that there are large areas of suitable land for afforestation and reforestation (in terms of being without encumbrance and with reasonably fast growth rates) in temperate North America, Europe, Australia, Chile, Argentina, Brazil and Uruguay. In Africa there are large areas of degraded savanna woodland, but this has lower yield potential and may not be unencumbered. It is important to keep in mind, however, that large areas of plantation may not be the best use of such land, especially from the standpoint of the needs of the people who presently occupy or use it. Any large scale afforestation or reforestation projects should be part of a land use plan, made with the full involvement of the people who depend upon the land.

There is also considerable potential for tree planting in homestead gardens, windbreaks and agroforestry systems (See question 58).

56. WHAT OTHER CONSTRAINTS ARE THERE TO LARGE SCALE AFFORESTATION INITIATIVES?

There are several other constraints to large scale afforestation initiatives in addition to the availability of land. These can be classified into four general categories; infrastructure, social, economic and ecological constraints.

INFRASTRUCTURE CONSTRAINTS - Limited institutional capacity, lack of research on appropriate species to plant, unrealistic government incentives, and soaring populations rates resulting in increased pressure on available land can constrain afforestation initiatives.

SOCIAL CONSTRAINTS - The interests and needs of local people living in areas proposed for afforestation are of paramount importance. When goals and objectives of forestry projects do not coincide with those of the local people, the results will be less than hoped for. Farmers can easily perceive government sponsored afforestation or reforestation efforts as an encroachment on customary land use rights and as a challenge to their welfare. Reactions of this nature have often led to active opposition and even sabotage through setting of intentional fires (Trexler et al 1992).

ECONOMIC CONSTRAINTS - Costs of afforestation programmes are highly variable, depending on the nature of the terrain to be planted, labour costs, and tree species to be planted. A rough global estimate indicates that tree planting costs can range from a low of $US 200 to a high of $US 2 000 per ha. Projected socio-economic benefits derived from plantations may not justify planting costs. (Bernthal 1990). Therefore it would be difficult, if not impossible, for countries receiving loans from development banks for afforestation projects to repay the loans.

ECOLOGICAL CONSTRAINTS - Ecological drawbacks to large afforestation projects include the potential for introducing low levels of genetic variability which can characterize large areas of single species plantations. This can reduce their resistance to site or climate related stress and (or) attack by insects and disease. Large scale forest plantings can also strain existing water resources in areas which are already experiencing overdrafts and escalating demands on ground water resources.

57. WHAT ASSISTANCE IS AVAILABLE TO SUPPORT AFFORESTATION AND REFORESTATION, PARTICULARLY AT THE INTERNATIONAL LEVEL?

Potential sources of funds include:

* National governments.
* International and regional development banks.
* Forest industrv.
* International donor agencies, e.g. UNDP.
* Bilateral donors.
* NGOs.
* Private enterprise.
* Public utility companies interested in offsetting carbon emissions

A large number of donors from the developed world, including international agencies, have extended financial support to establishment of forest plantations in the developing countries. The World Bank has financed forestry projects worth about $US 2.5 billion up to 1990. More than 50% of this amount has been used for plantation forestry (Pandey 1992). In 1990, development aid for the field of action "management of forests and plantations for industrial use" was $US 347.6 million or 25% of the total. This represents an increase of 1.8 times from the $US 191.9 million made available in 1988 (Ball 1992). It is worth noting, however, that the World Bank and many bilateral donors are making fewer concessionary loans or grants for industrial roundwood plantations, on the grounds that they should be profitable enough to seek support from normal funding sources.

The Global Environmental Facility (GEF), which is implemented by the World Bank, UNDP and UNEP, is a funding source which addresses four key environmental issues. These include reduction of GHG emissions, protection of biodiversity, protection of international waters and reduction in ozone layer depletion.

Another important component of afforestation and reforestation projects is technical assistance. This is also available through a number of sources including national governments, international technical assistance agencies such as FAO and international donors. An innovative programme to assist rural communities in developing countries to develop more effective strategies, methods and tools for forestry activities, including tree planting, is the Forests, Trees and People Program (FTPP). FTPP operates on the basis of a partnership between a community forestry team in FAO's Forestry Department in Rome and several national and regional institutions in Africa, Asia and Latin America.

58. HOW CAN AGROFORESTRY AND URBAN TREE PLANTINGS CONTRIBUTE TO THE MITIGATION OF CLIMATE CHANGE?

The magnitude of carbon storage contribution from agroforestry plantings will depend on the scale at which it is done and the ultimate use that is made of the wood.

Given suitable economic, social and environmental conditions, farmers have been found to adopt agroforestry systems readily. In countries where public forest lands are limited in extent or government tree planting efforts are limited, agroforestry plantings can represent a significant contribution to tree planting and carbon sequestration. There is a potential for increased forestry planting both in tropical and temperate zones. Large scale agroforestry tree planting schemes such as the "Four Around" schemes in China were reportedly carried out over 6.5 million ha of agricultural lands during the decade 1981-1990. A project of this magnitude, if successful, would sequester large amounts of carbon as well as providing other environmental benefits such as protection of soil from wind and water erosion.

Agroforestry systems are being considered in western Europe as an alternative intensive production systems which are currently in place that produce large surpluses of certain crops. In the Unites States, there are large areas which would benefit from increased windbreak and shelterbelt plantings (see question 55) (Sampson and Hamilton 1992).

Urban tree plantings would provide a more limited carbon storage benefit than rural plantings because by their nature, they would not be very extensive. However they have the potential to contribute other benefits in the climate change context which are much more significant (Fig 8.6). The effect of urban trees on local microclimates has undergone investigation during the past two decades, largely in developed countries. It is clear that urban trees have a significant and quantifiable effect on the immediate local climate and there have been various attempts to estimate what the effect of a major urban and community tree planting programme might be in the mitigation of carbon emissions. One estimate from the USA equates the planting of 100 million trees around homes, coupled with an effort to reduce heat absorption and radiation

Figure 8.6 - Shade trees, such as these neems planted along the streets of Niamey, the capital of Niger, lower temperatures and provide a more pleasant environment.

through a program of converting dark coloured surfaces, such as parking lots and buildings to light colours with a reduction of about 17 million tons of carbon from entering the atmosphere each year (Akbari et al 1988). Chinese urban foresters report that the climate of some cities have been markedly altered through widespread tree planting programmes (see box 8.1).

Trees can also have a significant beneficial effect on the cost of winter heating and summer cooling of buildings. Depending on its location, the energy conservation efforts of a single urban tree can prevent the release of 15 times more atmospheric carbon than it is able to sequester. Trees break up urban "heat islands" by providing shade. The shade provided by strategically placed trees per house can reduce home air conditioning needs by 30 to 50%. Trees planted as windbreaks around buildings in temperate and boreal regions can reduce winter heating energy use by 4 to 22%. Therefore urban trees offer a dual benefit of storing small amounts of carbon and protecting buildings from extreme hot and cold temperatures which results in lower consumption of fossil fuels. Urban tree planting may be especially beneficial in tropical regions where trees grow rapidly and the direct cooling benefits of shading are significant (Sampson et al 1992).

The effect of planting trees around buildings for energy conservation is sensitive to the type and shape of the tree involved, as well as its location. Deciduous trees that shade west-facing windows in the summer but allow solar radiation to strike the same windows in winter are especially desirable. In the northern hemisphere, trees on the south side of a house should be tall and fairly close to the house, with the lower boles pruned so that the winter sun can penetrate. For trees to be energy efficient, it is important that species, location and tree management be carefully and properly matched to the individual situation (Sampson et al 1992).

Box 8.1 Effects of tree planting on micro-climate in Nanjing, China

The industrial city of Nanjing, with a population of 1.5 million, is known as one of the five "furnace cities" of the Yangtze valley. Since 1949, some 3.4 million trees have been planted in and around the city with the specific objective of reducing summer temperatures and generally regulating the local climate, purifying the air and beautifying the environment. It is claimed that a drop in average summer temperature from 32.2° C to 29.4°C over the period 1949 to 1981 is directly attributable to the cooling effect of tree planting. Over 32 years, some 23 trees per inhabitant were planted. Tree plantings include block afforestation of degraded hillsides, windbreaks, triple rows of trees along railways and planting of street trees (Carter 1994).

59. IS THE PLANTING OF TREES SOLELY FOR CO_2 ABSORPTION A SOUND POLICY CONSIDERING OTHER NEEDS FOR AVAILABLE LAND?

There are many uncertainties presently associated with the global climate change issue. In addition, in many countries, the amount of land available that is suitable for agriculture and (or) forestry is limited. Therefore, any forest sector responses to adapt to or mitigate the potential effects of climate change should represent sound policy independent of predicted global warming and produce net benefits separate from those which may ultimately arise in the climate change context (e.g. timber, fuel wood, watershed protection, non wood products and non commodity values such as ecotourism and recreation). The position of FAO with respect to afforestation for CO_2 absorption is to encourage tree planting in areas where forest cover is the appropriate vegetation. This should be defined by land use plans and forest strategies as described in documents prepared under the Tropical Forests Action Plan (TFAP) and not by theoretical targets (FAO 1990) (see also question 45).

Instead of focusing narrowly on afforestation or reforestation, FAO supports the adoption of an integrated approach which includes:

* Management and protection of existing areas of natural forest to provide for long-term sustained yield productivity of a wide range of commodity and non-commodity resources including CO_2 absorption.

* Gradually increasing efforts in the afforestation or reforestation of appropriate sites with follow-up management and protection.

* Appropriate utilization of the wood produced to reduce the rate of carbon release.

60. WHAT FOREST POLICIES SHOULD BE CONSIDERED AT THE COUNTRY LEVEL TO ADDRESS THE THREAT OF CLIMATE CHANGE?

A policy aimed at reduction of current levels of **deforestation** and forest degradation should be of high priority in those countries where deforestation is a major activity. The implementation of such a policy will require actions in both the forestry and agricultural sector (see question 46). A policy of **afforestation/reforestation** is also warranted provided that it is **economically, ecologically** and **socially** sound, even in the absence of climate change considerations. Afforestation/ reforestation initiatives should be accompanied by policies and programmes designed to ensure the **health** of both plantations and natural forests so that the objectives of investments made in forest sector development will be met. A policy of **partial replacement of fossil energy sources by wood and other biofuels** is also worthy of consideration. Use of wood in place of materials from other sources whose production requires many times more energy contributes to energy savings, reduction of GHG emissions and to the maintenance of existing carbon reservoirs.

In developing forest sector policies to mitigate the effects of predicted global climate change, it must be recognized that these can **only** be done in concert with parallel measures to reduce fossil fuel emissions and to promote sustainable agriculture. Most of the present day contribution of greenhouse gases is the result of the burning of fossil fuels. Conservation of fossil fuels and the use of alternative energy sources, including the use of renewable energy sources is therefore, essential.

LITERATURE CITED

Akbari, H., J. Huang, P. Martien, L. Rainer, A. Rosenfeld and H. Taha, 1988. The impact of summer heat islands on cooling energy of consumption and global CO_2 concentration. in Proceedings of ACEEE 1988 Summer Study on Energy Efficiency in Buildings. vol 5, August 1988, American Council for an Energy Efficient Economy, 11-23.

Ball, J., 1992. Forest plantations and wise management of tropical forests. Proceedings of the Oxford Conference on Tropical Forests 1992, Oxford Forest Institute, UK, pp 97-109

Bernthal, F.M. ed, 1990. Formulation of Response Strategies. Intergovernmental Panel on Climate Change, Working Group III, WMO, UNEP, 257 pp.

Brown, S. and A.E. Lugo, 1982. The storage and production of organic matter in tropical forests and their role in the global carbon cycle. Biotropica 14:161-187.

Brown, S. and A.E. Lugo, 1984. Biomass of tropical forests: A new estimate based on forest volumes. Science, 223:1290-1293.

Brown, S., A.E. Lugo and J. Chapman, 1986. Biomass of tropical tree plantations and its implications for the global carbon budget. Canadian Journal of Forest Research 16:390-394.

Brubaker, L.B., 1975. Postglacial forest patterns associated with till and outwash in north central upper Michigan. Quat. Res. (NY) 5: 499-527.

Calabri, G. and W.M. Ciesla, 1992. Global wildland fire statistics. FO Misc/92/4, FAO, Rome, 48 pp.

Cane, M.A., G. Eshel and R.W. Buckland, 1994. Forecasting Zimbabwean maize yield using eastern equatorial Pacific sea surface temperature. Nature 370:204-205

Carter, E.J., 1994. The potential of urban forestry in developing countries: A concept paper. Forestry Department, FAO, Rome, Italy, 90 pp.

Ciesla, W.M., 1993. Supporting wildfire management worldwide. Stop Disasters 11:8-9.

Ciesla, W.M., D.K. Mbugua and J.G.D. Ward, 1994. Preliminary observations on dieback and mortality of *Juniperus procera* in Kenya. Integrated Forest Pest Management Centre, Ministry of Environment and Natural Resources, Nairobi, Kenya and Food and Agriculture Organization of the United Nations, Rome, Italy, KEN/91/005, Field Document 6, 11 pp.

Ciesla, W.M. and E. Donaubauer, 1994. Dieback and decline of trees and forests - a global overview. FAO Forestry Paper 120, 90 pp.

Coughlan, M.J. and B.S. Nyenzi, 1990. Climate trends and variability. In Climate Change, Science, Impacts and Policy, Proceedings of the Second World Climate Conference, Geneva, Cambridge University Press pp 71-82.

Cubash, U. and R. Cess, 1990. Process and modelling. In Scientific Assessment of Climate Change, IPCC WGI, WMO, UNEP, pp 75-98.

Davis, M.B., 1989. Lags in vegetation response to global warming. Climate Change 15:75-82.

Dixon, R.K., S. Brown, R.A. Houghton, A.M. Solomon, M.C. Trexler and J. Wisniewski, 1994. Carbon pools and flux of global forest ecosystems. Science 263:185-190.

Dykstra, D.P., 1994. Wood residues from timber harvesting and primary processing: A global assessment for tropical forests. Draft Working Paper, FAO, Rome.

Dykstra, D.P. and R. Heinrich, 1992. Sustaining tropical forests through environmentally sound harvesting practices. Unasylva 43/169:9-15.

Easterling, W.E., 1990. Climate trends and prospects. in Natural Resources for the 21st century, American Forestry Association, Washington D.C. pp 32-55.

Eriksson, G., G. Namkoong and J.H. Roberds, 1993. Dynamic gene conservation for uncertain futures. Forest Ecology and Management 62:15-37.

FAO, 1986. Wildland fire management terminology. Forestry Paper 70, FAO, Rome, Italy, 257 pp.

FAO, 1990. Climate change and agriculture, forestry and fisheries-Position paper. Second World Climate Conference, Geneva, Switzerland, 11 pp.

FAO, 1992. FAO yearbook of forest products. FAO Forestry Series No 125/FAO Statistics Series No. 103, FAO, Rome, Italy.

FAO, 1993. Forest resources assessment 1990 - tropical countries. FAO Forestry Paper 112, 59 pp + annexes.

FAO, 1994. Mangrove forest management guidelines. FAO Forestry Paper 117, 319 pp.

Finck, A., 1985. Nasse und trockene Sommer in früheren Jahrhunderten. Forschungsbericht und Halbjahresschrift der Universität Kiel, Heft 20 (neue Folge): 29-34.

Fosberg, M.A., J.G. Goldammer, D. Rind and C. Price, 1990. Global change: Effects on forest ecosystems and wildfire severity. in Fire in the Tropical Biota, Springer-Verlag, Berlin, pp 463-486.

Gable, F.J., J.H. Gentile and D.H. Aubrey, 1990. Global climatic issues in the coastal wide Caribbean Region. Environmental Conservation 17:51-60.

Global Environmental Change Report, 1994. Developing countries account for 37% of carbon emissions. 6:3-4, Cutter Information Corp.

Goldammer, J.G. and B. Seibert, 1990. The impact of droughts and forest fires in tropical lowland rain forests of East Kalimantan in Fire in the Tropical Biota, Ecosystem Processes and Global Challenges. Springer Verlag, Berlin, pp 11-31.

Gommes, R., 1980. Die Wetterlage im Laufe der Zeit. Zeitschrift für Geschichte, Folklore und Culture, 162-166.

Gommes, R., 1993. Current climate and population constraints on world agriculture in *Agricultural Dimensions of Global Climate Change*. St. Lucie Press, Delray Beach, Florida, pp 67-86.

Goodness, C.M., J.P. Palutikof and T.D. Davies, 1992. The nature and causes of climate change. Belhaven Press, London and Lewis Publishers, Boca Raton, 248 pp.

Grabherr, G., M. Gottfried and H. Pauli, 1994. Climate effects on mountain plants. Nature 369:448.

Grace, J., 1991. Vegetation and climate: a tenuous link in Modern Ecology: Basic and Applied Aspects. Amsterdam, Elsevier, pp 711-722.

Grainger, A., 1990. Modelling the impact of alternative afforestation strategies to reduce carbon dioxide emissions. Proceedings - Tropical Forestry Response Options to Climate Change, Sao Paulo Brazil, US EPA, pp 93-104.

Gray, W.M., 1993. Extended range forecast of Atlantic seasonal hurricane activity for 1994. Department of Atmospheric Science, Colorado State University, Ft. Collins, Colorado, 10 pp.

Hair, D and R. N. Sampson, 1992. Climate change - history, prospects, and possible impacts. in Forests and Global Change V. 1: Opportunities for increasing forest cover. American Forests, Washington D.C. pp 1-10.

Harrington, J. B., 1987. Climate change: a review of causes. Canadian Journal of Forest Research 17:1313-1339.

Hessburg, P.F., R.G. Mitchell and G.M. Filip, 1994. Historical and current roles of insects and pathogens in eastern oregon and Washington Forested landscapes. USDA Forest service, Pacific Northwest Forest and Range Experiment Station, Portland, Oregon, GTR 327, 72 pp.

Hepting, G.H., 1963. Climate and forest diseases. Annual Review of Phytopathology 1:31-50.

Hollinger, D.Y, J.P. Maclaren, P.N. Beets and J. Turland, 1993. Carbon sequestration by New Zealand's plantation forests. New Zealand Journal of Forestry Science 23: 194-208.

Houghton, R.A., 1990. Projections of future deforestation and reforestation in the tropics. Proceedings - Tropical Forestry Response Options to Climate Change, Sao Paulo Brazil, US EPA, pp 87-92.

Houghton, J.T., 1991. Scientific assessment of climate change: Summary of the IPCC Working Group 1 report. Proceedings Second World Climate Conference, Geneva, Switzerland, Cambridge University Press, pp 23-46.

Hutacharern, C, K.G. MacDicken, M.H. Ivory and K.S.S. Nair, 1990. Proceedings of the IUFRO workshop on pests and diseases of forest plantations. FAO, Regional office for Asia and the Pacific, RAPA publication 1990/9, 283 pp.

IPCC, 1992. The 1992 IPCC Supplement, WMO/UNEP, 70 pp.

IPCC, 1994. Summary for policymakers of the 1994 WG I report on radiative forcing of climate change. WMO/UNEP, IPCC 10th Session, Nairobi, Kenya IPCC X/Doc 3 Part 1, Item 3.1.

Izrael, Y.A., M. Hashimoto and W.J. McG. Tegart, 1990. Potential impacts of climate change. Intergovernmental Panel on Climate Change, Working Group II, WMO, UNEP, pp 39-40.

Jacobson, J.S. and A.C.Hill ed, 1970. Recognition of air pollution injury to vegetation: A pictorial atlas. Air Pollution Control Association, Pittsburg, Pennsylvania, USA.

Karekezi, S., 1994. Household energy initiatives for a sustainable future. Foundation for Woodstove Dissemination, Nairobi, Kenya, Stove Notes 10, 35 pp.

Kristiansen, G., 1993. Biological effects of climate change: An introduction to the field and survey of current research. Global Change and Terrestrial Ecosystems, International Geosphere-Biosphere Program.

Lanly, J.P., 1982. Tropical forest resources. Forestry Paper 30, FAO, Rome 106 pp.

Lanly, J.P., 1989. Forest resources of the world. Proceedings Wildland Fire Conference, 23-26 July 1989, Boston, MA, USA, USDA Forest Service, pp 10-13.

Lashof, D and D. Tirpak, 1989. Policy options to stabilize global climate. U.S. Environmental Protection Agency, Office of Policy Analysis. Washington D.C.

Lincoln, D.E., N. Sionit and B.R. Strain, 1984. Growth and feeding responses of *Pseudoplusia includens* (Lepidoptera: Noctuidae) to host plants grown in controlled carbon dioxide atmospheres. Environmental Entomology 13:1527-30.

Lincoln, D.E., 1993, Herbivore responses to plants grown in enriched CO_2 atmosphere. in Global Change Research: Summaries of Research in FY 1993. US Dept Energy DOE/ER-0597T, pp 112.

Lugo, A.E. and S. Brown, 1992. Tropical forests as sinks of atmospheric carbon. Forest Ecology and Management, 54:239-255.

Maunder, W.J., 1990. The climate change lexicon (Provisional Edition). Second World Climate Conference, Geneva, Switzerland, 131 pp.

McGovern, T.H., 1991. The economics of extinction in Norse Greenland. in Climate and history: Studies in past climates and their impact on man. Cambridge University Press, pp 404-433.

Miller, W.F., P.M. Dougherty and G.L. Switzer, 1987. Effects of rising carbon dioxide and potential climate change in loblolly pine distribution, growth, survival and productivity. in The Greenhouse Effect, Climate Change and U.S. Forests. The Conservation Foundation, Washington DC, pp 157-189.

Ministère de l'Agriculture et de la Pêche, 1994. La gestion durable des Forêts Francaises. Direction de l'Espace Rural et de la Forêt. 76 pp.

Mueller-Dombois, D., 1992. Potential effects of the increase in carbon dioxide and climate change in the dynamics of vegetation. Water, Air and Soil Pollution, 64:61-79.

Mueller-Dombois, D. and J.G. Goldammer, 1990. Fire in tropical ecosystems and global environmental change: An introduction in Fire in the Tropical Biota, Ecosystem Processes and Global Challenges. Springer Verlag, pp 1-10.

Olson, J.S., J.A. Watts and L.J. Allison, 1983. Carbon in live vegetation of the major world ecosystems, US Dept Energy, Oak Ridge National Laboratory, Oak ridge, Tennessee, USA ORNL 5862.

Pandey, D., 1992. Assessment of tropical plantation resource. Swedish University of Agricultural Sciences, Department of Forest Survey, 128 pp. (Prepared within the framework of the FAO 1990 Forest Resources Assessment Project).

Parry, M.L. and T.R. Carter (ed), 1984. Assessing the impact of climate change in cold regions. Summary report SR-84-1, International Institute for Applied Systems Analysis, Laxenburg, Austria, 42 pp.

Patterson, D., 1993. Did Tibet cool the world? New Scientist 139:29-33.

Pearce, F., 1994. Forests destined to end in the mire. New Scientist 140:16

Pearce, F., 1994. Not warming, but cooling. New Scientist 143:37-41.

Peters, R.L., 1990. Effects of global warming on forests. Forest Ecology and Management. 35:13-33.

Pinard, M.A., 1994. Reduced-impact logging project. ITTO Tropical Forest Update 4:11-12.

Plass, G.N., 1959. Carbon dioxide and climate. Scientific American 201: 41-47.

Pollard, D.F.W., 1985. A forestry perspective on the carbon dioxide issue. Forestry Chronicle, August: 312-318.

Putz, F.A., 1994. Towards a sustainable forest. ITTO Tropical Forest Update 4: 7-9.

Sampson, N. and T. Hamilton, 1992. Can trees really help fight global warming. American Forests 98:13-16.

Sampson, R.N., G.A. Moll and J.J. Keilbaso, 1992. Opportunities to increase urban forests and the potential impacts on carbon storage and conservation. in Forests and Global Change, American Forests, Washington D.C., pp 51-67.

Sarimento, J.L., 1993. Atmospheric CO_2 stalled. Nature 365:697-698.

Sauerbeck, D. R., 1992. Potential impacts of climate change on agricultural production. Institute of Plant Nutrition and Soil Science. German Federal Research Center of Agriculture, Bundesallee, Braunschweig, Germany, 15 pp.

Schroeder, P., 1991. Carbon storage potential of short rotation tropical tree plantations. US EPA, Corvalis, Oregon, 19 pp.

Sedjo, R.A., 1990. The global carbon cycle - Are forests the missing sink? Journal of Forestry 88:33-34.

Sedjo, R. and A. Solomon, 1989. Climate and forests. Paper prepared for workshop on controlling and adapting to greenhouse forcing, EPA and NAS, Washington DC, 14-15 July 1988.

Seigenthaler, U. and E. Sanhueza, 1990. Greenhouse gases and other climate forcing agents. in Scientific assessment of climate change. Intergovernmental Panel on Climate Change, Working Group 1, WMO, UNEP, pp 47-58.

Solomon, A.M. and P.J. Bartlein, 1992. Past and future climate change: response by mixed deciduous-coniferous forest ecosystems in northern Michigan. Canadian Journal of Forest Research 22: 1727-1738

Sombroek, W.G., 1990. Soils on a warmer earth: The tropical regions. in Soils on a warmer earth, Elsevier, Amsterdam, pp 157-174.

Sombroek, W.G., 1991. The greenhouse effect, plant growth, and soils. Soils Reference and Information Center (ISRIC) 91/45 3 pp.

Sombroek, W.G., F.O. Nachtergaele and A. Hebel, 1993. Amounts, dynamics and sequestering of carbon in tropical and subtropical soils. Ambio 22:417-426.

Stine, S., 1994. Extreme and persistent drought in California and Patagonia during medieval time. Nature 369:546-549.

Stommel, H. and E. Stommel, 1983. Volcano weather. Seven Seas Press, Newport, RI, USA, 177 pp.

Trexler, M.C., C.A. Haugen and L.A. Loewen, 1992. Global warming mitigation through forestry options in the tropics. in Forests and Global Change, American Forests, Washington D.C., pp 73-96.

USDA, 1988. Forest health and productivity in a changing atmospheric environment, a priority research program. Forest service, Forest Fire and Atmospheric Sciences Research Staff, Washington D.C., USA, 56 pp.

USDA, 1994. America's forests: 1994 health update. Forest Service, Agriculture Information Bulletin 696, 20 pp.

Watson, R.T., H. Rhode, H. Oeschger and U. Sieganthaler, 1990. Greenhouse Gases and Aerosols. in Scientific Assessment of Climate Change. Intergovernmental Panel on Climate Change, Working Group 1, WMO, UNEP, pp 1-44.

Wertman, J., 1976. Milankovitch solar radiation variations and ice age ice sheet sizes. Nature 261:17-20.

Windelius, G. and P. Tucker, 1990. The sun, sovereign ruler with chilling power: an assessment of the potential impact of solar activity on future climate. Unasylva 41/163:15-21.

Winjum, J.K., R.K. Dixon and P.E. Schroeder, 1992. Estimating the global potential of forest and agroforest management practices to sequester carbon. Water, Soil and Air Pollution 64:213-227.

WMO, 1994. Drier forests in prospect? World Climate News, 5:5.

WRI, 1990. World Resources 1990-91: A guide to the global environment. Oxford University Press, New York.

Zimmerman, P.R., J.P. Greenberg, S.O. Wandiga and P.J. Crutzen, 1982. Termites, a potentially large source of atmospheric methane, carbon and molecular hydrogen. Science 218:563-565.

INDEX